A VERY GOOD GOD IN A BADLY BROKEN WORLD

DAN BOONE

THE FOUNDRY
PUBLISHING

Copyright © 2019 by Dan Boone
The Foundry Publishing
PO Box 419527
Kansas City, MO 64141
thefoundrypublishing.com

978-0-8341-3786-8

Printed in the
United States of America

Cover design: J.R. Caines
Interior design: Sharon Page

Library of Congress Cataloging-in-Publication Data

A complete catalog record for this book is available from the Library of Congress.

10 9 8 7 6 5 4 3 2 1

Dedicated to my departed friend Millard Reed.
You complained well to a God who is hard to explain.
And you still loved this God to the core of your being.

CONTENTS

ACKNOWLEDGMENTS

I owe this book to people whose pain I wish had never occurred. I was with them when the unthinkable happened. And I was often in the room when sloppy explanations of God were offered by well-meaning people who have never experienced the darkness that can hide the face of God. I write this book for them and with them, and maybe for you. But I also write it for a world that seems to have gone crazy with mass shootings, bombings, and random destruction. How do you explain a good God in such a world?

So, whether you are a person with hard questions for God, or a person wondering if God is in the present chaos, I pray these old texts will knock on your door and find you at home. Today I am remembering:

- A murder-suicide in North Carolina that left three little children to be fought over in court—and me explaining to a judge why they should not go to the family in our church.
- The sudden death of Tom, the patron saint of the church, who picked up the trash in the ditch in front of the church and who loved my family dearly.
- Debbie, who lost her husband, and then her son, and then her father.
- Louise, whose mother was raped and murdered.

- The slow, agonizing death of Julie, one of the finest Christians I've known (I still have questions about her death, and I complained to high heaven about having to be nice to God at her funeral).
- A college student, Heather, who sat on our living room floor every Sunday night until she was killed in an accident, leaving the other twenty college students questioning.
- A train that wrecked in Bourbonnais, Illinois, affecting a town with loss and grief.
- The death of Josh, a very young child, and Marcus, only a baby, and the twins, James and John, who were both killed in the same wreck.
- Larry, who died like the vibrant Christian he was—but his healed life would have been better.
- A mosquito bite that took the coordination and mental awareness of Don and Becky's son and left them with a life of care-giving.
- Nicole, who died in a wreck, ending her dreams of being a medical missionary.
- Robin, who died of alcohol consumption down by the river. We did all we knew to keep him away from booze. He was the best soccer coach in town, the friendliest greeter at the church door, and the life of the neighborhood.
- Ashley, my daughter's freshman roommate, who died in her twenties.

These I can name. I cannot begin to name the many people who lost loved ones to gun violence, schools who lost their innocence in brutal attacks, families affected by the chaos of mental illness, and towns that are marked forever by horrible evil that happened within their city limits. I cannot name all the injustices that have wrecked the lives of our next-door neighbors.

People do dark deeds. Some even get away with it. Even though others face consequences, the scars they inflicted never seem to heal. It raises questions about a just and loving God. Added to the personal darkness is a corporate darkness, resulting in poverty, racism, sexual harassment, hatred, castigation, and division. Much of this has now spilled into the church of Jesus, where fellow "saints" treat one another like bitter enemies in the name of political ideology. The rants on social media are causing many to ask, "Where is God in all this?"

Across the years, I have been in the trenches where humans deal with this darkness, both personal and corporate. I'm sure the grace of God has permitted me to forget many of the tragedies and hurts. But I cannot forget the questions. Most, I have no answer to. I've simply collected them and added mine to them. These friends have helped me write this book. Were it not for them, I would not be familiar with the darkness that hides the face of God.

I also wish to express appreciation to a man I never met but of whose writing I am deeply appreciative. The late Eugene Peterson shaped my approach to ministry. I think I have read every book and commentary he wrote. But my deepest appreciation for him rises from his translation of the Bible, The Message. He gave us the poetry of the Bible in our own words and expressions. His work in Job and the Psalms is soul language at its honest best. He expresses the pain of humans in language that grips us. I highly recommend spending a year reading through The Message. I have used his paraphrase for most of the scriptures you find in this book. Thank you, my published friend.

We will visit three old friends from Scripture: the writers of the Psalms of lament, Noah, and Job. We will sit at their feet and learn from their suffering. We are not worthy to tie their shoes but, nevertheless, have been invited to sit quietly before their haunting questions and expressions of pained humans. Maybe there is more grace in the darkness than we dreamed.

Finally, I am thinking about Millard Reed, who was my Bible quizmaster, a pastor after whom I modeled my ministry, my predecessor in the role of university president, and my friend. After his retirement, he lived near the campus of Trevecca Nazarene University. Every day he made his way to the cafeteria to eat with colleagues. Then he walked down to Trevecca Health Care Center to sit with his wife, Barbara. She had not known him for years—Alzheimer's. Occasionally, he got a smile or a word that contained some faint hint of recognition. We didn't really know. After a life of stellar service to God, I wanted better for my friend in his retirement. While God's grace is obvious, a loving wife who was present would have been a better blessing. And for Millard, Parkinson's disease caught up with him. He lived his last days in the same room with Barbara. With grace-filled humility and a diseased body, he taught me how to finish well when it isn't going well. The last time I visited him, he asked me to tie his shoes. I dedicate this book to him.

Dan Boone

PART 1
THE STORY OF NOAH

We often keep only the ending of a story in our memory. With Noah, we are left with an interesting ark, animal pairs, a rainbow, and a promise that the earth will never again be destroyed by the waters of primordial chaos. Archaeologists have searched for the big boat, and some have claimed to find it. A Christian amusement park in Kentucky has built a replica. Kids have asked curious questions. Were there dinosaurs on the ark? How did they keep the snakes in their cage? Who fed the lions? If they sacrificed some of the animals as soon as they hit dry ground, are they extinct today?

The one thing we have not done is think about the character of the God who was behind this massively destructive divine decision. What does this reveal about God? And, given that the flow of Scripture places this story immediately on the heels of creation itself, how do things go so wrong so fast?

Our world is swamped in chaos. Maybe this is a good moment for us to visit an old story and figure out what God is up to when we are bobbing for our lives in the tide of global evil and personal tragedy.

1 | OVEREHEARING THE REGRET OF GOD

IT WAS A whisper spoken in the privacy of their bedroom. The boy who had given them fits had become a man. He had rebelled, disobeyed, disrespected them. And now, with his recent violence, he had broken his parents' hearts. His latest crime had gone beyond broken rules—he had left broken bodies. His parents were in their bedroom talking. The lights had long been off; sleep was long past due. He was out there somewhere, still doing violence to people. One parent whispered words of anguished regret: "I wish we'd never had him." If the boy had been standing there, had overheard the whispers of his grieved parents, would it have made any difference?

That's the question we are faced with in the story of Noah and the ark. In this well-known, well-loved story, we are brought face to face with the regret of God. We overhear God say, "I wish I'd never made them"—and he's talking about you and me.

Our story does not begin with regret. It begins with the words, "God saw that it was good" (see Genesis 1). God is pleased with his creation and his creatures. God and the humans stroll the garden and discuss horticulture and animal monikers. They share common interests in work and play. They take the same break at the end of each week. They are partners in creation. Humans are the epitome of God's handiwork. God has made space in the universe for the existence of will other than his own will. Humans are free and empowered to cooperate with God in the management of the world. It is good—very good.

But in Genesis 3, things begin to unravel in a terrible way. Eve sees something she wants and seizes it. Adam follows suit. No longer satisfied with their partnership with God, they wish to be self-sustaining, independent creatures. They will fend for themselves now that they know good and evil. They run and hide, and in hiding, they discover their desire to cover themselves before God and before each other. It is no longer safe to be naked in the world.

Curses follow: Eve bears babies in pain; Adam farms fields in sweat; the ground grows weeds. They're a long way from the idyllic garden-tending arrangement they began with. And the worst is yet to come: Eve gives painful birth to two boys, one of whom eventually murders the other. More babies are born, and evil multiplies exponentially across the earth. God's vision of a good creation is going downhill faster than a Disney roller coaster.

Genesis 6 begins with one of the weirdest stories in the whole Bible. The sons of God look down on the daughters of humans and are captivated by their beauty. They see what they want and seize it, just like Eve did with the forbidden fruit (it's the same Hebrew word). The result of their offspring is a race of warriors—people skilled at killing each other. Cain's murderous art has been perfected by this marriage between the sons of God and the daughters of humans. And, with eternal blood in them, there will be no end to the murderous deeds of humankind. At this point in the story, God limits human life to 120 years; God caps evil.

The next words in the story may well be some of the most sobering in all of Scripture: "The LORD saw that the wickedness of humankind was great in the earth, and that every inclination of the thoughts of their hearts was only evil continually. And the LORD was sorry that he had made humankind on the earth, and it grieved him to his heart. So the LORD said, 'I will blot out from the earth the human beings I have created—people together with animals and creeping things and birds of the air, for I am sorry that I have made them'" (Genesis 6:5–7, NRSV).

We're on page 5 of a 1,009-page story called the Bible, and the main character is having second thoughts. In five pages we've gone from "God saw that it was good" to "God saw and regretted." The word used to describe the grief in God's heart is the same word used for the pain in the woman's womb—the curse has gotten into God. God's creatures are seeing and seizing, and they are destroying the earth. Violence (*hamas* in Hebrew) covers the earth. Humans cannot transcend their self-interest to care for one another. I'd always thought of the story of Noah and the ark as a good story about animal pairs and rainbows in the sky—but not anymore. It is the story of God's regret. It is the story of a dark moment when God decides to act on his regret and wash us all away.

God-talk interests me. My friends often speak of God in mechanical, preplanning ways. They recount these opening chapters of the story of humanity like this: *Before God made Adam and Eve, he already knew they were going to make a royal mess of things, but he went ahead and made them anyway. After they misbehaved, he slapped a few curses on them to let them know they couldn't get away with such behavior. Then he kicked them out of the garden to give them a taste of the world on their own. Things got worse, but God wasn't worried. He just sent a catastrophic flood to get everyone's attention. Then he preserved the memory of the flood in an ark. Noah made sure everyone who came after the flood knew about the time God got sick and tired of humans messing up his world.* That's how I hear people tell this part of the story—mechanical. No surprises. God arranged it all beforehand. God lined up the dominoes and let them fall. But I have trouble with that way of telling the story.

One Christmas, our family got hooked on dominoes, and we learned a game called Mexican Train. You pile the dominoes in the middle of the table and each player draws fifteen dominoes. To start the game, you place the double-twelve in the middle of the table. Each player then starts his or her own train off the double-twelve, matching to it one of their own dominoes that has a twelve on one end. The strategy is to continue to line up your dominoes on your own train by matching the numbers on the ends of the dominoes, connecting them in one straight line. You alone can play on your train. You hope to play each domino in order—but there are ways to mess people up. Someone can play a double on their train and leave it open, which means the next person has to cover the open double before he or she can play anywhere else. People start groaning when they have to pull one domino from the middle of a perfectly arranged train waiting to be played; now there is a gap in their numerical sequence. When it happens to you, your train has been derailed by a rogue double—your competitor has messed up your train.

As I read Genesis 6, I see that God hadn't counted on the mess we made. It wasn't preplanned. God wasn't tipping dominoes by himself; God was playing with partners. And when we played rogue dominoes on our train, God had to respond. This isn't how God intended the game to go. As I read the text, I see that, had God known in Genesis 1:1 what he knew in Genesis 6:5, he never would have emptied the box onto the table. Like the parents whispering in the bedroom, he wished we'd never been born.

Denise and I have been privileged to enjoy watching our daughters act in dramatic performances. I remember when Abby was in the high school's production of Agatha Christie's *Arsenic and Old Lace*. I knew the plotline. I'd seen the play before. I wouldn't be holding my breath to see how it turned out. But if I were reading the Bible for the first time and came to the Noah story on page five of holy Scripture, I'd be thinking some serious thoughts about the characters. These humans really are free to wreak destruction, and so is God—only, God is a lot better at blotting out.

The freedom of God is more frightening than the freedom of humans. God is on the verge of giving up his vision for a partnership. God is grieved deeply and regrets having ever made us. God is deciding to pull the plug on the universe. God is vulnerable to the evil we do. God can be pushed too far.

Did you know that?

2 THE BATTLE BREWING IN THE HEART OF GOD

IN THE ANNALS of human accounting, there are more than 250 ancient flood stories. The most famous account, other than the Genesis rendering, is the *Epic of Gilgamesh*. Those Babylonians could weave a tale. Their story was well known at the time Genesis was written. The similarities between their story and ours are remarkable. But I'm not nearly as interested in the similarities as I am in the differences. Anybody can copy. It takes a creatively novel viewpoint to differ.

In the *Epic of Gilgamesh*, the flood occurs because the gods are at war. The gods of destruction are pitted against the gods of preservation. Like a World Wrestling Federation grudge match, the gods in this story vie for control of the universe. The chants in the crowd rise.

"Save!"
"Destroy!"
"Save!"
"Destroy!"

Winner takes all. Humans are left to feebly cheer for the gods of salvation and to guess how they might appease the saving gods.

In the biblical story, we also find a battle brewing. But this battle rages in the heart of the one true God, maker of heaven and earth. We see deeply into the regretful grief of our God, who utters both words, "save" and "destroy." The crisis in this story is not an apocalyptic ending of the world as we know it. The character of God is at stake.

This is not the only time God will teeter on the seesaw of decision between salvation and destruction. After Moses leads the Israelites out of Egypt, God calls Moses to the mountain to reveal how free people are meant to live. While Moses takes legal dictation on top of Mount Sinai, the liberated people down below are dancing around a golden calf, pledging themselves to this "god" who brought them out of Egypt. When Moses returns to camp, God is angry at the sight and tells Moses to stand aside. "Destroy" is about to trump "save." Moses reminds God that God has a reputation to uphold. What will the Egyptians say? That God brought them out into the wilderness to destroy them? God relents and limits the destruction while saving the community.

Another time, in the book of Hosea, God sues for divorce from Israel. They are adulterous to the core. The papers are filed. The case of marital unfaithfulness is airtight. Israel has no loophole to slip through. But, just before the gavel comes down to end the relationship, God changes his mind. *"How can I give you up? How can I treat you like everyone else?"* The save-destroy dilemma continues.

In these two stories, God decides to save. But in the Noah story, God decides to destroy. The words are chilling: "I will blot out from the earth the human beings I have created . . . for I am sorry that I have made them" (Genesis 6:7, NRSV). We can't believe our ears. At least with the gods of salvation in the *Epic of Gilgamesh,* we had a fifty-fifty chance. In the story of Noah, when God decides to destroy, there is no other power to whom we can appeal.

Then from absolutely nowhere, without buildup or introduction, Noah enters the story. He's almost an afterthought. The only mention of him has been his birth announcement in Genesis 5:28–29. His father, Lamech, "named him Noah, saying, 'Out of the ground that the LORD has cursed this one shall bring us relief from our work and from the toil of our hands'" (v. 29, NRSV). Noah sounds more like a union rep than a savior of humankind. His name means "rest." And on the heels of God's decision to blot out every living creature comes a terse announcement that Noah found favor in the eyes of the Lord. The God who sees universal violence also sees a righteous man named Noah. He's a married father of three boys who all have wives. Noah walks with God. Noah is blameless. That's about all we get on Noah.

Most storytellers try hard to make him the hero of the story. But Noah is a flat character. In literary terms, he's a foil: a character to whom other characters react in order to reveal their own character. Noah has no lines.

Zero. Noah never speaks. He listens to long speeches made by God. Noah never emotes. We are never told how he feels about the information he is being given. It doesn't even say that Noah is the *only* righteous man left. For all we know, there were others to choose from. So we are left to guess why God sees Noah and is pleased.

Maybe Noah is a good listener. That would make him rare in the eyes of God. Most of us go blabbering away about everything we need God to do for us. Noah seems to be a man of few words. God is probably tired of hearing human drivel.

Maybe Noah is a good carpenter. Probably an early forerunner of the Amish. Good with his hands. Builds things that last. That would come in handy—but that presupposes that God has already decided to save a remnant of humanity.

Maybe Noah doesn't have a type-A personality. He wouldn't steer too much. After all, the ark is a flotation device that's going nowhere specific. It just floats.

Maybe Noah won't freak out at the announcement that God is about to blot out every living thing on the earth. I've known a few people like that—cool, calm, collected when everything is coming apart around them. It would take a man of that constitution to live in cramped quarters with relatives and animals for most of a year.

The story doesn't waste words telling us why Noah. Maybe Noah had been talking with God all along about how bad things were. Maybe God found Noah to be good company. I'm guessing they shared a similar vision for the world and the same pain in their gut.

The introduction of Noah is the only word of hope in the story up to this point. Apart from Noah, there is no future. I'm still shaken by God's capacity for destruction.

Who's to say God won't regret again? I know about the rainbow at the end of the story. I know about God's promise to never again destroy the earth—*by flood*. But there are other ways. Greenhouse gases. Polluted water. Atomic, nuclear, or dirty bombs. Terrorists. Planes flown into buildings. Asteroids. Global warming. Drought. Biological weapons. A virus. Or, God could just remove grace from the planet and watch us do each other in.

It makes me wonder what God is whispering in heaven's bedroom these days. God has watched the world grow and change for a long time now. And God has seen plenty. We've filled a river in Rwanda with 800,000 dead bodies from a tribe we didn't like. We've played retaliation in the land of Jesus's birth, each side trying to out-kill the other. We've watched nations sanction ethnic cleansing. We've elected leaders who kill without remorse. We've cloned animals and (allegedly) humans and no longer need God now that we have our own specs. We've spent enough on lawn fertilizer in the United States to feed entire starving nations. We've aborted, euthanized, and warehoused people. We've libeled, sued, and backstabbed. We've spread disease around the world. We've polluted the world with American "entertainment." We've turned women and children into sex toys. We've ignored the pleas of persecuted peoples. We've raped the planet of its natural resources without regard for those who come after us.

Who's to say God won't look down once more and regret making humankind on the earth? If humans are free to cover the earth with violence, why is God not free to respond with greater force?

3 | CREATION IN REVERSE

THE ARK is about a football-field-and-a-half long. Three decks with stalls for animal pairs. Food storage bins. Made of teak or gopher wood. Coated with pitch inside and out to keep it from leaking. Side entry. Skylight on the roof.

The word in Latin means "box" or "chest." It isn't a word used for nautical vessels. It's what you store things in. My wife's grandfather had a trunk that he brought over from the old country. He stored his valuables in it. It sits in our living room today, holding our keepsakes. We've never considered it a flotation device.

The ark has no steering mechanism. It isn't designed to go anywhere. Like a rubber ducky, it simply floats, bobbing up and down in the water. God is the architect of this floating box. Noah is its builder. And God decides to store God's keepsakes in the box. Two of every creeping thing, animal, and bird. God wants male and female. God collects clean and unclean. God keeps two of everything—which should say something to us about God's intent that we live in relationship. The God about whom we cannot talk without meaning Father, Son, and Spirit is a God of interdependence. The saved creation is to be a relational and varied creation. The box holds zebra, flamingo, copperhead, box turtle, barn owl, cricket, hyena, groundhog, gray squirrel, and more. Creation in a keepsake box. Waiting for rain. Hoping to be saved.

Then God acts on the divine pain in the gut. The deluge begins. God tips over the heavenly rain barrel and pours water down. God pulls his finger from the subterranean dike below and water gurgles up. Down like cats and dogs. Up like bubblin' crude. It rains for forty days and nights.

Forty is an important biblical number. It is usually viewed as a time of testing. Forty days of rain to test our capacity to dog-paddle. Forty years in the wilderness to test an unbelieving generation out of business. Forty days without food to test Elijah's deep depression. Forty days for Jesus in the wilderness to see if Satan could put a better offer on the table. Forty days is about how long it takes for us to realize that we're in a mess we can't get ourselves out of.

It rains for forty days and nights. This is more than a bad weather pattern or an extraordinarily rainy season. This is the creation story in reverse. These are the same chaotic waters that God drove back in Genesis 1. These are the deep and dark waters that covered the face of the earth. These are the waters that God pushed back to make room for creeping things, fish, fowl, and us. If you want a narrative on the progress of the flood, read Genesis 1 and 2 backward. Breath leaves. Humans and animals die. Vegetation shrivels. Dry land disappears. Darkness reigns again. The God who blew the waters of chaos back now holds his breath and lets them return. The God who breathed life into nostrils, now doesn't. "Everything on dry land in whose nostrils was the breath of life died" (Genesis 7:22, NRSV). It hurts to say it.

Knowing that forty is the limit of testing, we have some expectations when the rain stops. Things should take a turn for the better. Noah has done everything the Lord commanded him to do. The pitter-patter ends. Now what? Isn't this where the good part comes? Our Bible stories tell us that when the testing stretch of forty ends, Canaan is conquered, birds bring food to Elijah, and Jesus emerges victorious. This is the post-forty payoff we are led to expect.

But Noah and his family wait. No word from God. So they wait some more. Their homes are gone. Their farms are sea bottom. Their neighbors are all dead. What's to go home to?

They wait another forty days. And another forty days. And another forty days. Certainly by now God is satisfied with the demise of creation. Isn't this overkill? And they wait another thirty days.

It's now been 150 days since the rain stopped. And the text records soberly, "Only Noah was left, and those that were with him in the ark. And the waters swelled on the earth for one hundred fifty days" (7:23–24, NRSV).

How long is 150 days? A lot longer than 40. It's about the average time it takes for career turnover following a company shutdown. It's about the length of a problem pregnancy. It's about the time it takes to run through a few rounds of radiation and chemotherapy. It's about the time it takes for a divorce to run through the legal system and split what God joined together. It's about the time it takes for a bad influence to begin to get under your skin. It's a season of drought. It's a run-up to a war. It's a kid going bad. It's a disease being fully discovered. It's depression setting in. One hundred fifty days is more than a month but less than half a year.

I have to wonder what Noah is thinking. He has no lines in the story, so we don't know. I'm guessing he feels as vulnerable as a leaky knothole. All it would take would be an outbreak of a virus or a charging rhino. He must be feeling both vulnerable and forgotten. That's how I'd feel after 150 days. After 40 days, I'd feel tested. After 150 days, I'd feel forgotten. Does Noah ever lean against gopher wood and ask, "God, have you forgotten us?" We don't know.

But we do know that others have asked that same question. The children down in Egypt wondered it: has God forgotten us? Barren Hannah wanting a baby asked it: has God forgotten me? Blind Samson, post-haircut, weak and tied to a pole as a laughingstock asked it: have you forgotten me? Job asked it.

The exiles in Babylon asked it. Jesus asked it. And I'm guessing Noah asked it.

I read a series of stories written by people who had experienced the equivalent of Noah's 150 days. Jerry Porter wrote about the death of his daughter, Amy, who lost a courageous fight against cancer as a young adult. Brent Cobb, a missionary to Korea, wrote of the excruciating death of his six-year-old son, who was playing near an electrical transformer when it blew up. David Best wrote about the chaplains of New York City following 9/11. One story placed two people side by side: Stan Meek and Bev Williamson. They had the same disease and the same faith but different outcomes. One was miraculously healed; the other died. Donna Gilbert wrote about her son with autism, Sean. Fletcher Tink told the story of Ruth Benites, whose husband, Hersey, was the forty-fourth pastor assassinated in Bogotá, Columbia, in a five-month period—about 150 days. I wonder how many of these writers asked, "Lord, have you forgotten me?"

Forty days of testing is one thing; 150 days of lonely vulnerability is quite another. Perhaps you've been there. Destruction all around. Barely afloat. Boxed in. Patching leaks. Supplies dwindling. Cramped quarters. Nothing to go home to. No steering mechanism. Dead in the water. It probably feels like God has pulled the plug on creation.

4 WILL YOU REMEMBER ME?

AS A UNIVERSITY PRESIDENT, I get my fair share of farewells. Every year, the seniors leave in May. Relationships change as cars and U-Hauls head out from the campus in every direction. These are sentimental moments of parting. Life will never be the same again for that group that shared the third floor of Johnson Hall or Benson Dorm. They vow to stay in touch. Sometimes they choose a song. For several years, it was "Friends Are Friends Forever," which is a great song, but its shelf life was short. Soon came a song that vowed then asked, "I will remember you. Will you remember me?"

We want to be remembered. Of all the things humans fear, one of the greatest is that we will be forgotten. We fear we will live, strive, work, play, love, build, give, sweat, sing, care—and no one will remember. It scares us.

This fear is heard in the cries that have risen: Remember the Alamo! Remember Pearl Harbor. Never forget 9/11. Something happened to our fellow humans that we do not want to forget. We want to be remembered. It's why we built memorials at Normandy and Nagasaki. It's why people's names are engraved at the Vietnam Memorial and the Holocaust Museum. It's why they begin memorial services in Oklahoma City and New York with the reading of a very long list of names. Someone is waiting to hear each name. It's why pews and Bibles have names written on them and in them. In the human heart is the deep fear of being forgotten. In each deed of remembering others, we are tacitly hoping that we too will be remembered.

She called the church sobbing. The secretary couldn't quite make out who it was, so the call was passed on to me. Between sobs I heard her say, "You remembered." One of our pastors had delivered a rose to her home that morning. It was our way of commemorating the first anniversary of a death. Her husband had died a year ago on that day. We remembered.

In the Bible, the flood is a device for forgetting. It is a means by which God can blot out the creatures who have brought grief and regret to his heart. God is an ark away from having no living reminder of the humans who filled the earth with violence. The lone carriers of human memory are bobbing in a box on the dark waters of death. Memory hangs by a fragile thread.

When I talk with new Christians, they often tell me that they find the God of the New Testament much more kind than the God of the Old Testament. I understand how they come to that conclusion, especially when they read the story of Noah. God is trying to eliminate us from the face of the earth and leave no trace of evidence that we were ever here and no witnesses to tell the story of how we died. If that is your introduction to God, trusting does not come easily.

One of the missing elements of the Noah story is the account of the victims of the flood. There are no reports from the drowned. They never speak. They give no opinion. They register no protest. They are not standing in line in the rain to file grievances at the local courthouse. They are not clawing at the door wanting in. They leave no message in a bottle. They are forgotten. I think this is one of the reasons this story registers so deeply in our minds. We are reading this story and wondering about them. Were they given every chance to repent? Was a prophet sent to warn them? Did they go straight to hell? Might Jesus have visited them during his three-day jaunt to the grave to offer them a second chance? Were they all equally guilty? Was Noah really the only righteous one on the entire planet?

I could go on. You could too! We are defending human memory. We are asking that these flood casualties be remembered because we are afraid *we* will be forgotten. If God can blot out these without a trace, what guarantees do we have?

If you hit the pause button at the end of Genesis 7, you have Noah and the lone survivors waiting for a word from God. It has been 190 days since they came on the ark and endured 40 days full of rain followed by 150 days of silence from God.

We are contemplating a future void of Abraham, David, and Ezekiel. No Hun, Hitler, or Hussein. No Mary and Joseph, and therefore no Jesus (because Jesus is just as much Mary as he is God). No Billy Graham or Mother Teresa. No Ralph at the gas station or Patty at the coffee shop. No you. No me.

And the next line in the story says, "But God remembered Noah and all the wild animals and all the domestic animals that were with him in the ark" (Genesis 8:1a, NRSV). Noah was God's investment in memory. Noah was God's forget-me-not. Noah would tell the story about God's regret and God's destruction. Noah would preserve the memory of the drowned. God remembered Noah.

This is not a story about bad humans. It's a story about a God who, try as he might, cannot forget his creation. God does not have it in his character to blot us out and walk away. Even at the height of our evil, we cannot exhaust the saving will of God.

God remembers. The flood story isn't the only place we see it. In the days of Babylonian exile, God's people are far from home. God's judgment on them is the reason they are there. God has dealt with them by allowing a pagan army to flood their land and wash them away to Babylon. These displaced people are convinced that God has forgotten them. Babylon is as foreign and forgotten as the ark.

And God says, "Can a woman forget her nursing child, or show no compassion for the child of her womb? Even these may forget, yet I will not forget you. See, I have inscribed you on the palms of my hands" (Isaiah 49:15–16a, NRSV).

And God says,

> For your Maker is your husband, the LORD of hosts is his name; the Holy One of Israel is your Redeemer, the God of the whole earth he is called. For the LORD has called you like a wife forsaken and grieved in spirit, like the wife of a man's youth when she is cast off, says your God. For a brief moment I abandoned you, but with great compassion I will gather you. In overflowing wrath for a moment I hid my face from you, but with everlasting love I will have compassion on you, says the LORD, your Redeemer. This is like the days of Noah to me: Just as I swore that the waters of Noah would never again go over the earth, so I have sworn that I will not be angry with you and will not rebuke you. For the mountains may depart and the hills be removed, but my steadfast love shall not depart from you, and my covenant of peace shall not be removed, says the LORD, who has compassion on you.
> (Isaiah 54:5–10, NRSV)

God remembers. It does not mean that God is blind to our sin or that he looks the other way when we do violence. But it does mean that God cannot forget us.

At the birth of Jesus, Luke measures the moment in song. Mary sings about the Lord who has remembered to be faithful to Israel according to the promise made to ancestors. In the next chapter, Zechariah sings about the Lord who has remembered the holy covenant and the mercy promised to the ancestors.

God acts in ways that keep memory alive. Without Noah, there would be no singing from Mary or Zechariah. And we're still singing—because God remembers.

5 | THE SIN-CONSEQUENCE MACHINE

I TEACH PREACHING. Sometimes I wonder if that is possible. Preaching is such a strange thing to do. One human dares stand before other humans and speak what God is saying through Scripture to the gathered community. I am hesitant to stand up and preach. One writer called it a sweet torture. So I teach people to sweetly torture themselves by stepping into a pulpit.

Of all the skills I try to teach, the most important one is paying attention to the text. We Americans have been educated to master texts. We conquer material in textbooks and spit it back on exams to the people who forced our nose in the book.

When we read Scripture, we are like the *Star Trek* crew of the USS Enterprise, scanning the alien vessel for signs of life and activity. This approach to Scripture places us in the driver's seat. We scan, master, and conquer. Then we preachers declare what we have mastered to the waiting congregation.

And I think this is all wrong.

When we position ourselves before Scripture, we are not in the driver's seat. We are not meant to master but to be mastered by God. We are not meant to conquer but to be conquered by the Word that is sharper than any two-edged sword. We are not meant to scan but to become aware that we are being scanned by the Word that penetrates even to the gap between joint and marrow, soul and spirit.

The first move in preaching is to place ourselves under the Word of God and allow God to do with us as God pleases. We do this by asking questions. The three questions that get me under the text most quickly are these:

1. What are humans doing?
2. What is God doing?
3. How are humans responding to what God is doing?

When I read the Noah account, the answers are readily apparent. Humans are filling the earth with violence. God is blotting out these humans, except for Noah's floating zoo. Humans respond after the flood by continuing to do the same evil they did before the flood. The before-and-after pictures of humans show little improvement. Prior to the flood (Genesis 6:5), the Lord saw the great wickedness of humans on the earth and the evil inclinations of their hearts. After the flood (Genesis 8:21), the inclinations of the hearts of humans are still evil from youth.

If the flood is a story about changing humans, the whole attempt is a washout. We didn't change. For proof, keep reading in the text. In just a few chapters, you'll find Noah drunk and naked in his tent. (Maybe we should cut him a little slack since he was cooped up in a smelly boat for a whole year with in-laws and the largest zookeeper's duty of all time. Those conditions might drive anyone insane.) A few chapters later, humans are building a tower to the heavens—just in case God floods the place again? Read on. Jacob lies to his father and manipulates his brother. Aaron leads worship around a golden calf. King David has his eye on another man's wife. Jezebel is running the Holy Land. People are bringing their half-dead, scrawny animals to sacrifice to God (instead of the best of their herds). The religious leaders can't recognize the Messiah even though he's right under their nose. Judas betrays Jesus. The Corinthians are doing foul things. The church at Laodicea makes God sick to his stomach. And these are the characters in the *good book*.

The flood doesn't change us. But it does change God. Before the flood, God was sorry that he made humans and decided to wipe us out. After the flood, God vowed never again to use a flood to destroy all flesh, and he laid down law calling for respect of life. We go from "I will blot out" to "Never again!" We go from "I will destroy" to "I will make a covenant." The flood is a story about a change of heart in God.

What has changed? God has responded to the reality that humans are violent. God has decided that immediate retribution will no longer be the way of dealing with our evil. God has chosen to ally himself in covenant with his cantankerous partners. God has decided to bear the pain of our wickedness. God has chosen to participate in the pain of the world rather than wipe it out. God has chosen to redeem the world through suffering love rather than erase it from memory. God has chosen to allow that which is radically other to exist. God has chosen to allow rebels to go on breathing. God has decided not to be a sin-consequence machine.

The flood was about swift, immediate retribution. We sinned, and God dished out the consequence. Just like a judge in a court, a parent with a paddle, a quarter in a vending machine, we got what was coming to us. God no longer operates in that mode. God has changed.

I think lots of us have forgotten this story. We see our world filled with violence and cry out for God to do something. We want God to make the bad people go away. Take out the terrorists. Execute the murderers. Lock up the criminals. Fire the jerks. Wash out foul mouths with soap. In other words, we are asking God to revert to the pre-flood arrangement. We want the sin-consequence machine back again. But God said "never again," which is both very good news and very disheartening news. Jesus was telling us the truth in Matthew 5:45 when he said that we are followers of a Father who "makes his sun rise on the evil and on the good, and sends rain on the righteous and on the unrighteous" (NRSV). God is kind to the wicked.

During February 2003, I found myself thinking a lot about Saddam Hussein. He had murdered thousands of his own people and threatened the world with his use of power. The whole civilized world was debating what to do with this murderer. I found myself wondering if I could have killed him. Given the opportunity, could I take him out? I decided that I could.

I remembered Dietrich Bonhoeffer, the famous German pastor and theologian who participated in an attempt to assassinate Hitler. The plot failed, and he was imprisoned. Days before the liberation of the camp where he was held, the Nazis hanged him. Bonhoeffer was trying to do the world a favor. Had he succeeded, I wonder how he would have lived. Could he then consider taking out other evil people? Could he do the world other 'favors'? Where would one stop if one began to rid the world of violence and evil? And if I had taken out Saddam, where would I stop?

Maybe those who do these things also have to die, lest the temptation be too great.

If God were to change his mind and become a sin-consequence machine again, I am confident of one thing: God would not stop where you and I would stop. God sees all evil in every form. The execution of justice would be complete and thorough. Do you want that?

Some say yes. They are confident that they would be Noah, righteous enough to be on the salvation boat. "Bring it on," they'd say. They believe they could meet the standard and face the flood of judgment.

And they would be wrong. And their theology would be very bad because their hope of being saved would be resting on—well, their own righteousness and their belief that they are sufficiently wise to judge others.

I don't think I'd be standing. I keep finding inclinations in my heart that I need saving from.

I suppose we ought to listen carefully to the text. It intersects our community. If the flood causes God to abandon a sin-consequence response, maybe we should too. Don't you think?

Jesus, help us love our enemies.

6 WHY ARE THERE SO MANY SONGS ABOUT RAINBOWS?

God emerges from the flood offering covenant. "When the bow is in the clouds, I will see it and remember the everlasting covenant" (Genesis 9:16a, NRSV). The God whose heart was moving away from his creation is now moving toward it. Five times the narrator presents a God who says, "Never again."

I've said those words plenty of times to God. As a young teen, I beat a path to the altar of the local church. I think I owe them for carpet. Each time I'd promise God never again to do the thing I had promised last time never to do again. I became eloquent in my promises. Each "never again" had to be equal to or better than the last one. Certainly God was recording these. I promised to read my Bible every day and to pray. I promised to witness to Dickie Bennett. I promised to stop thinking sexually about girls. I promised to study harder and make an A in algebra. I promised to treat my sisters more kindly. All eloquent promises. All eloquently broken.

God's eloquence was a rainbow. And God only spoke it once. Everything since has been a reminder. And the rainbow wasn't even for us. God is reminding God about God's promise. God said, "I will see it and remember."

Apparently the promises that matter are not the ones we make to God but the ones God makes to us. I'm not saying God isn't interested in whether we keep our word. What I'm saying is that the hope of our salvation is in God keeping God's word. There has to be a steady hook to hang a rainbow on. And our promises don't hold in thin air.

Maybe when we pray, God isn't looking for us to make eloquent promises about what we are and aren't going to do. Maybe God wants us to hear the divine promise that offers us a covenant relationship that we didn't and don't deserve. Maybe God wants us to stop betting our life on our power to keep our promises and start betting our life on God's power to keep God's promises. Rainbows remind me that God has been doing a good job.

All this talk about God makes it sound as if humans have nothing to do. When it comes to our salvation, we don't. We're in over our heads. God alone provides salvation. Our expertise is in filling the earth with violence. God's expertise is in saving such critters.

We have nothing to add to our salvation. But there is something we can do in response to God's saving activity. As soon as Noah's feet hit dry ground, he built an altar. He took some of the animals God had saved and offered them as a sacrifice back to God. (I personally wish Noah had sacrificed the mosquito and the gnat.) Here he is, taking the very life that God has painstakingly saved and offering it up in total sacrifice. The only way to respond to being saved from sure death is to give your life to the one who saved you. Noah built an altar, offered a sacrifice, and pleased God (Genesis 8:20–22).

Salvation, like a knee tapped with a reflex hammer, initiates a response. We call this response *the sanctified life*. It is a life saved by God, hallowed by God, lived toward God. Salvation profoundly changes us into beings who respect life the way God respects life, who love enemies the way God loves enemies, who care for the earth the way God cares for the earth, who suffer the pain of evil in the world the way God suffers the pain of evil in the world, who desire peace the way God desires peace, who move to heal brokenness the way God moves to heal brokenness.

Our life business is the business of God. Once we disembark from the ark, we have no other reason for living. Ours is a holy vocation from this moment on. If we go on destroying and killing, it is our own doing, not God's. The biblical word for this arrangement is "covenant." God offers Noah and his family covenant. There are no conditions, but there are responsibilities once we have offered ourselves to be part of the covenant. The heart of the covenant is that we are to behave like God—a tall order.

One of my favorite words in the Bible is the Hebrew word *chesed*. It is the term for covenant faithfulness and loyalty. I always talk about *chesed* at weddings. A relationship is beginning that will be severely tested. I want the couple to know that God is establishing *chesed* between them. It means that each of them has the right to expect certain behavior from the other in light of the promises they are making on this day.

That's what God was doing with Noah. God was saying, *You have the right to know something about me from this day on. I am binding myself to you, even if you fill the earth with violence. I am committing to participate in my creation, to enter it by means of those through whom I can savingly work. I will never again throw in the towel. When I am angry, my judgment will be leveraged to save. When it rains like cats and dogs and you wonder if it's going to keep pouring down for forty days and nights, just keep looking up. At the end of the rain, you'll see the rainbow, which is my way of saying that I remember. You have the right to expect saving behavior from me in light of the promises I have made to you.*

God has kept *chesed* with us even though we have not made it easy. One dark night, we arrested the God-become-flesh Jesus. He came to share in our human condition, but we viewed him as a threat. We went to a garden and arrested him. We beat him, convicted him with a stacked jury, mocked his royalty, and forced him to drag his own cross through our streets. We spit on him. We nailed him up and stripped him naked for the world to see. We killed the God who came to redeem our violence.

If ever there was a day that God wanted to renege on the promise made to Noah, I think it could've been that day. We were at our violent best. And the sky did darken. Clouds did form a ceiling over our wicked heads. But the rain never came. God stayed faithful to the promise. God entered into our sinful suffering and died in the place where we die.

I suppose that's why there are so many songs about rainbows.

PART 2
THE STORY OF JOB
LED BY SUFFERING TO THE HEART OF GOD

Our eyes rush to scriptures of grace, mercy, and forgiveness—as Pollyanna might call them, the happy texts. We love the steadfast love of God shown to thousands of generations, the grace of the God and Father of our Lord Jesus Christ, the fellowship of the Holy Spirit. These texts lift an inch off the page and beg our attention. They make us feel good about life.

Other biblical themes barely make a peep—ideas like fiery judgment, jealous God, and punishing children to the third and fourth generations. The people of Scripture who experienced the death of every first-born child in Egypt, fire and thunder on Mount Sinai, and the slaughter of idol worshipers in the wilderness believed God to be capable of wrath and darkness. They had no doubt regarding God's capacity to vent. Their God is hard to explain.

While we wish to ignore these parts of Scripture, we cannot. The Bible is as full of holy terror as it is tender love. And in the world we live in, where terrorism is a horrifying reality, depicting God as a terrorist is not advantageous for the seeker-sensitive church working hard not to offend. How do we speak of this God to a generation raised on 9/11, ISIS, and mass shootings? These texts are not good PR for God.

How do parents wrap their brains around a God who asks Abraham to roast his only son in one Testament and sends the divine Son to a cruel crucifixion in the other Testament? How does a world of rampant individualism find any justice in sin being punished three and four generations later? Few of us wish to be God's spokesperson answering for actions we took no part in. It is a dreadful thing to fall into the hands of a living God. Welcome to the story of Job!

One of the ways we try to deal with these texts of terror is to suggest that those who obey God are "terror-exempt."[1] The commandments seem to suggest that the obedient get steadfast love for a thousand generations and the disobedient living hell for three or four generations. But when we widen the scope of the biblical narrative, we have Noah standing in the rain shaking his head, Job scratching his boils, and

1. Barbara Brown Taylor, "Preaching the Terrors," *Leadership Journal* (Spring 1992), 43. See the entire article for an excellent review of preaching biblical texts of terror. *Leadership Journal* was published by *Christianity Today*, where the article's archive can be found: https://www.christianitytoday.com/pastors/1992/spring/92l2042.html.

friends from the psalms of lament uttering the unthinkable. These, and so many others in our biblical narratives, confirm our fear that saints suffer—sometimes horribly. Even Jesus. Our book has frightening things in it, and we cannot explain them away, which also means that our God is radically different and cannot be predicted or understood by the creatures he creates. We stand before him in awe.

I took my granddaughter to the pizza establishment Chuck E. Cheese's, an indoor carnival of games, shows, and not-so-good pizza. Chuck E. is a costumed seven-foot-tall rat who prowls around the place high-fiving kids and having fun. But when Anna Ryan, age three, saw him, she retreated in horror and latched herself to my leg with a death grip. No explanation could shake her loose. "He's just a nice man in a suit. It's not real; it's just a costume. Look, all the other children are playing with him." Wasted words on a child who had no frame of reference for a seven-foot-tall rat that walked among mere babes.

To be encountered by a God of unexplained motives causes us to clutch all the more tightly to our fixed ideas about who God is and how God operates. We prefer a settled God who is predictable in every way, not one who prowls among weaklings with the power to crush.

Maybe the terror texts do their work when they unsettle us. Maybe we are meant to be aware that we are in the presence of One for whom there is no frame of reference, and to whom nothing can compare. Maybe we are supposed to realize that our God is not a stranger to judgment, violence, terror, and death. Maybe we are supposed to think about the long-term effects of our sin. Maybe the texts still drive us toward the God whose mystery is magnetic.

Anna finally likes Chuck E. She has gotten used to him—almost. I asked her recently about going to Chuck E.'s place. She thought for a minute and said okay. Her hesitation caused me to ask her what she thought about the rat. Her reply was sacred.

"I'm still just a little bit scared."

Not a bad posture to assume before the God of terrors.

7 WHEN GOD REMOVES THE HEDGE

SOMETIME in your life you will probably suffer. Some great pain will flood your life with sorrow and agony. You will not understand why, and though you'll look for a reason, you will not find one. We are wired to want answers. That's why books about suffering are so popular:

When God Doesn't Make Sense, by James Dobson in 1993

When Bad Things Happen to Good People, by Harold Kushner in 1981

Where Is God When it Hurts, by Philip Yancey in 1977

The Problem of Pain, by C. S. Lewis in 1940

Many of us who are followers of God wish there were simple answers because we've been cornered by doubters who nail us with their questions: How can a God of love let people be killed in gas ovens at Dachau? How can you explain the Oklahoma City bombing or the Twin Towers? And, much closer to home, what about Dave, Josh, and Mary?

We cannot explain why. We float our guesses, but it doesn't stop the questions. Nor does God pipe in with help. There is an awkward silence.

Suffering strips away the veneer of life. We learn that we are not as secure as we thought. We ask, "Why me?" Some of us go through our lives with a fine-toothed comb, looking for transgressions that could possibly make us deserving of the blow we've received. Suffering changes the way we see the world, and it shatters certain kinds of faith. We talk about God, or don't talk about God, in ways different than we did before.

Job understands. If you come to his story wanting simple answers, prepare to be disappointed. Getting inside Job is a little frightening—like a seven-foot-tall rat to a little girl. But the God who is silent for most of the book will speak, finally—though not convincingly enough to settle the matter. There are still questions about the power of God.

People who have survived hurricanes like Katrina, Sandy, Harvey, and Irma can tell you stories about the destructive power of water. Hurricanes in the United States have collapsed dams, washed away levies, overrun sandbags, consumed houses with floodwaters to the roof. In most of the places where hurricanes have struck, there were hedges of protection set up to guard against the destructive power, yet these safeguards have proven futile time and time again. Water can take everything in its path, and it will send the wise in search of higher ground.

The people of Noah's day had no ground that was high enough, no safe turf to which to flee. A flood became the instrument of God's judgment on their sin. And the flood was simply creation without the hedge of God's protection. God stepped aside and allowed chaos to do what it does best: destroy life. God removed the hedge of protection in Noah's day.

That's what also happened to Job. A flood came crashing down on him. According to the story, God moved the hedge and let it happen.

The story begins with God bragging about Job as upright, blameless, devout, the greatest man among the people of the East, a righteous man with a fully devoted heart, a man of integrity. This is Billy Graham, Mother Teresa, and Saint Francis of Assisi all rolled into one holy person. This is not just a nice guy; this is the most righteous man on all the earth. And God is the one saying all these good things about him. Read with me from The Message's translation of Job 1:8-12:

> God said to Satan, "Have you noticed my friend Job? There's no one quite like him—honest and true to his word, totally devoted to God and hating evil."
>
> Satan retorted, "So do you think Job does all that out of the sheer goodness of his heart? Why, no one ever had it so good! You pamper him like a pet, make sure nothing bad ever happens to him or his family or his possessions, bless everything he does—he can't lose!

But what do you think would happen if you reached down and took away everything that is his? He'd curse you right to your face, that's what."

*G*OD *replied, "We'll see. Go ahead—do what you want with all that is his. Just don't hurt* him." *Then Satan left the presence of G*OD.

God accepts Satan's challenge. I'm not sure I'd want God betting on me. But God believes Job's righteousness is deeper than trinkets and treasures. God decides to give Job the terrible dignity of proving that his integrity runs deeper than what he gets from God. Right off the bat in the book of Job, we are given to understand that God is not about utilitarian religion, or religion for reward. There is actually something satanic about serving God for what we can get. To serve God for reward, insurance, blessing, or a protective hedge is to fall short of knowing God as God wishes to be known. This makes God into an idol to be appeased for the goodies.

God refuses to let such a claim stand. Satan says Job is righteous because God has built a hedge around him. God says no. Let's see.

The story plays out in a three-tiered universe. In heaven above, God and Satan converse. On earth, Job lives with his wife, children, and friends. In Sheol below, the dead are unconscious in the grave.

We tend to read the account from an earthly perspective, where Job and his friends are talking about his suffering. We ask earthly questions. Why do bad things happen to good people? What are the causes behind human suffering? But these are not the main questions of the book. The story is told in answer to a simple question: *why is Job righteous?* The readers of the book want to know if Job's trust in God is linked to a divine hedge of protection. They want to know what Job will do if the hedge is removed. How will he speak of God, to God, about God? What will become of his integrity? We may wish to change the focus to other issues, but this is the heart of the narrative.

So God removes the hedge. In our story, God is sovereign. Satan cannot operate without permission. God is free to do as God pleases without needing permission from anyone. God removes the hedge. God allows Job's suffering. The Old Testament man was correct in understanding that, ultimately, both good and evil and come from the hand of God, whether by cause or permission.

We've done our human best to protect ourselves from catastrophe: security alarms, insurance policies, neighborhood watch, health checkups, nest eggs, airbags, steel bars, passwords, identity protection, and armed forces. And most of the time, our hedges hold. We are mindful to have good, thick hedges. As Christians, we half believe that, if we serve God, our families will be protected and our homes secured from danger. We'd like to believe that being in church every week gives us a better chance at escaping calamity. But there are too many among us who have gotten positive test results back, buried children, lost jobs, had our hearts broken. And we know that "hedge religion" is not foolproof. But we wish it were. And if it were, Satan would be right. We'd do it for what we get back in return.

God removes the hedge around Job. And the Sabeans raid Job's oxen. Lightning strikes Job's sheep and shepherds. The Chaldeans steal Job's camels. A tornado kills Job's children. In rapid-fire order he is reduced to nothing. His business? Gone. His possessions? Gone. His children? Gone.

Job's response (1:20–22) was orderly and appropriate:

Job got to his feet, ripped his robe, shaved his head, then fell to the ground and worshiped: "Naked I came from my mother's womb, naked I'll return to the womb of the earth. GOD gives, GOD takes. God's name be ever blessed." Not once through all this did Job sin; not once did he blame God.

God is winning the wager so far. The hedge is gone, and Job has not cursed God. He is grieving, yet he clings to his integrity.

In chapter 2, God is bragging again. This cannot be good for Job. Look at verses 1–6:

One day when the angels came to report to GOD, Satan also showed up. GOD singled out Satan, saying, "And what have you been up to?" Satan answered GOD, "Oh, going here and there, checking things out." Then GOD said to Satan, "Have you noticed my friend Job? There's no one quite like him, is there—honest and true to his word, totally devoted to God and hating evil? He still has a firm grip on his integrity! You tried to trick me into destroying him, but it didn't work."

Satan answered, "A human would do anything to save his life. But what do you think would happen if

*you reached down and took away his health? He'd
curse you to your face, that's what."*

*GOD said, "All right. Go ahead—you can do what you
like with him. But mind you, don't kill him."*

Does Job's integrity end at his own skin? Is he the kind
of God follower who can handle anything exterior but
collapses when it gets under his own hide? The hedge
shrinks. Job's body becomes vulnerable to disease.
The only thing left guarded is his very life. Verses 7–8:

*Satan left GOD and struck Job with terrible sores.
Job was ulcers and scabs from head to foot. They
itched and oozed so badly that he took a piece of
broken pottery to scrape himself, then went and sat
on a trash heap, among the ashes.*

We want to ask how God can let this happen to a
good man like Job. But heaven is asking, "How will
Job speak of God now? Will Job bless God after this?"
The issue is his righteousness—in the Hebrew, *tamim*,
meaning "upright, innocent, whole, internally coher-
ent." It is what holds Job together.

Verses 9–10:

*His wife said, "Still holding on to your precious in-
tegrity, are you? Curse God and be done with it!"*

*He told her, "You're talking like an empty-headed
fool. We take the good days from God—why not
also the bad days?"*

*Not once through all this did Job sin. He said noth-
ing against God.*

Many have followed the advice of Job's wife. They de-
manded an answer and didn't get one. They felt cheat-

ed, abandoned by God. And they turned and walked away. Job gives an incredibly pious answer: "I didn't complain when goodness came from God's hand, so why should I complain when trouble comes from the same hand?" Be careful not to paint Job as stoic, however. Within a few chapters he will be questioning God, yelling at God, trying to sue God, and accusing God. But he never curses God. For now, he sits on the ash heap of social rejection with all the other failures and losers—the cursed folk. Another biblical character, Jesus, will suffer in a similar place.

Job's friends come. Like good friends, they sit with him for seven days in silence, which is quite remarkable, if you ask me. Most friends of religious persuasion burst through the door muttering some theological explanation. Job's friends simply sit and say nothing. And then Job himself speaks in 3:3-10:

Obliterate the day I was born. Blank out the night I was conceived! Let it be a black hole in space. May God above forget it ever happened. Erase it from the books! May the day of my birth be buried in deep darkness, shrouded by the fog, swallowed by the night. And the night of my conception—the devil take it! Rip the date off the calendar, delete it from the almanac. Oh, turn that night into pure nothingness—no sounds of pleasure from that night, ever! May those who are good at cursing curse that day. Unleash the sea beast, Leviathan, on it. May its morning stars turn to black cinders, waiting for a daylight that never comes, never once seeing the first light of dawn. And why? Because it released me from my mother's womb into a life with so much trouble.

After cursing the night of his conception and the day of his birth, he asks questions, all beginning with the word "why." *Why* didn't I die at birth? *Why* did my mother feed me? *Why* did I ever see the light of day? *Why* does God bother to keep such miserable people alive? But then Job asks the most piercing question of them all in verses 23–26:

What's the point of life when it doesn't make sense, when God blocks all the roads to meaning? Instead of bread I get groans for my supper, then leave the table and vomit my anguish. The worst of my fears has come true, what I've dreaded most has happened. My repose is shattered, my peace destroyed. No rest for me, ever—death has invaded life.

Job prefers never to have been born at all, or to have died instantly at birth. He prefers an unconscious grave to this earthly existence. There are things that can hurt so bad that we wish we'd never been born. Job is there. His outcry is the honest eruption of a suffering soul whose seven silent days on the ash heap have finally led to questions. Something has been shattered inside Job. His trust in God is now brought into the conversation. He has progressed from "God gives, God takes. God's name be ever blessed" in 1:21 to "He said nothing against God" in 2:10 to "My repose is shattered, my peace destroyed. No rest for me, ever—death has invaded life" in 3:26.

For Job, the world can never be the same again. He can never speak of God in the same way again. What form of righteousness will rise from this ash heap? What does shattered faith look like? How do hedgeless people talk about God? Is there a future in God for those who suffer innocently?

Satan watches.

God trusts Job.

Job wants to die—or at least get some answers.

8 WHEN THERE ARE NO ANSWERS

THOSE OF US who have lived awhile have learned some things by trial and error. We've watched humans behave and have drawn conclusions. Certain actions result in certain consequences. The fool and his money are soon parted. The one who sows wicked deeds reaps wicked consequences. The one who cares for a tree will eat its fruit. Cause and effect. You reap what you sow. You get what you deserve. We believe this, and we want our children to believe it. We want them to wise up and listen to us because we know the consequences of their bad choices. We know where the moral boundary lines are drawn. We know what people ought and ought not to do.

And besides, it's scriptural. The Proverbs are a fine collection of this type of observed wisdom—cause-and-effect religion. Deuteronomy is a narrative masterpiece of this theology. Obey God and you will inherit the land, produce bountiful crops, drink from choice wells, and have lots of kids. You'll be heaven-blessed. But disobey God and you'll pay a hefty price. You'll get drought, blight, enemies pestering you, childlessness, and poverty aplenty. With cause-and-effect religion, good things happen to good people and bad things happen to bad people. God as much as guarantees it in Proverbs and Deuteronomy.

And then something happens that makes no sense. We did good and got bad. Or even worse, the guy who did bad got good.

Job doubts what he has always believed to be true and is groping his way toward a new knowledge of God. He is entertaining the thought that God may not be as cut and dried as he thought. Job has lost his business, his possessions, his kids, his social standing, his reputation, and his health. He's sitting atop an ash heap scraping sores and wrestling with cause-and-effect religion. Maybe God has a dark side, mysterious and wildly free.

Job has friends who've come to help. They live like Job has always lived up until now. They haven't suffered. But they've come to fix their pal Job. After listening to his soliloquy, they begin. They offer the Scriptures, the tried and true texts of cause-and-effect religion. They've quoted this party line all their lives and it's always been enough to quell doubt. The only explanation for Job's plight is that Job has sinned—big time. He's been bad, real bad. And he is reaping what he has sown. "Repent, Job! Change your wicked ways! God will be good to you if you do!"

But Job, being the man of integrity that he is, knows he has done nothing wrong, nothing to deserve this type of treatment from God. He says so. His friends don't believe him. Their theology has only one explanation for this calamity: sin.

Job's friends scare me. I'm afraid I might look in the mirror and see one of them. I can be so sure about God's ways and God's doings. I have my theology down pat, tightly woven, no loopholes, airtight. I can explain to you why things happen to certain people.

- "I saw it coming 3 years ago."
- "I knew she was a flirt and that this would come back to haunt their marriage."
- "I can tell you his problem—he's too liberal."

We're so sure. We know about people, don't we, friends of Job? And if they'll give us half a chance, we can fix them. We know how. Our formula works.

- Pray this prayer.
- Read this book.
- Go to this seminar.
- See this counselor.
- Memorize these verses.
- Listen to this preacher.

Job refuses to be fixed by the religion of his friends. He refuses to be fixed because his authentic experience does not fit their theology. They think he sinned. He knows that sin has nothing to do with this. He calls them names: windbags, sorry comforters. He's not getting by with a little help from his friends. Instead, in chapter 6, he challenges them. Verses 14–30:

When desperate people give up on God Almighty, their friends, at least, should stick with them. But my brothers are fickle as a gulch in the desert—one day they're gushing with water from melting ice and snow cascading out of the mountains, but by midsummer they're dry, gullies baked dry in the sun. Travelers who spot them and go out of their way for a drink end up in a waterless gulch and die of thirst. Merchant caravans from Tema see them and expect water, tourists from Sheba hope for a cool drink. They arrive so confident—but what a disappointment! They get there, and their faces fall! And you, my so-called friends, are no better— there's nothing to you! One look at a hard scene and you shrink in fear. It's not as though I asked you for anything—I didn't ask you for one red cent—nor did I beg you to go out on a limb for me. So why all this dodging and shuffling?

Confront me with the truth and I'll shut up, show me where I've gone off the track. Honest words never hurt anyone, but what's the point of all this pious bluster? You pretend to tell me what's wrong with my life, but treat my words of anguish as so much hot air. Are people mere things to you? Are friends just items of profit and loss?

Look me in the eyes! Do you think I'd lie to your face? Think it over—no double-talk! Think carefully—my integrity is on the line! Can you detect anything false in what I say? Don't you trust me to discern good from evil?

Joseph Cardinal Bernardin wrote a God-anointed book in the last days of his battle with the cancer that claimed his life. In it he wrote, "Whenever we are with people who suffer, it frequently becomes evident that there is very little we can do to help them. . . . The reason this is so frustrating is that we like to be 'fixers.' We want not only to control our own destiny, but also that of others."[1] My experiences with those who have suffered tell me that it is cruel to interpret their suffering via our own explanations. I think Cardinal Bernardin was right. We know we do not have control of our friends' suffering; therefore, neither do we have control over our own uncertain futures. The security of our hedge is also in question.

We must be merciful toward fixers who have not yet suffered. Their cause-and-effect faith has gotten them where they are. They are enjoying their health, homes, jobs, business success, educational attainments, and reputable friends. They accept all this as the gift of God that it is. They believe it to be either the wink of God's approval on their righteousness or a blessing with no other explanation but God. But in the grand scheme of the God-Satan wager, Job's friends are betting with Satan. They say Job was good because God protected and blessed him and that if Job will just repent to get back in God's good graces, he'll be restored and get his stuff back. But God has given Job the terrible dignity of proving them all wrong.

1. Joseph Louis Bernardin, *The Gift of Peace: Personal Reflections* (New York: Doubleday, 1998), 47–48.

Whom are you cheering for? I think we want Job's friends to be right. Then we can look across the fence at the family whose kids are turning out badly and we can be assured it's because they didn't take them to church—and be equally assured that our kids will turn out just fine because we rarely miss church. We can look at folk who are sick and know they just didn't eat right, while reminding ourselves of the care we take in our diets. We can conclude that the poor are poor because they are lazy, while knowing we'll always have enough because we work hard—and tithe. And the kids who have no honor roll bumper stickers to grace their parents' cars? Well, they just didn't apply themselves like ours did.

And maybe every bit of this is true! Could it be that sometimes, most of the time, cause and effect *is* right? Could it be that Proverbs and Deuteronomy explain life *most of the time*? Could it be that this *is* a good way to raise children, work, eat, study, run a business, and live?

Job's friends are partly right. There are consequences for behavior, rewards for discipline, and punishments for sin. This is the way of God. But it doesn't always explain every situation. God cannot be boxed in or universally predicted, especially when people suffer.

Job actually wishes his friends were right because, then, the solution would be easy: an apology from God. When it dawned on God that Job had not committed grievous sins, God would come down with a sheepish grin on his face and say, "Job, old buddy, old pal, I owe you an apology. I wasn't paying attention the other day when some nasty stuff got labeled with the wrong address, and I'm here to make it up to you because I know you did nothing to deserve this. You've been a faithful and loyal servant, and I'm going to see to it that nothing like this ever happens to you again. I've fired your guardian angel."

But we never hear God say, "Oops." The language of Job toward God in chapters 3–37 is blunt, brutal, and accusatory. Repeatedly, the friends try to reel him in and change his mind about why this has happened to him. But Job is not buying it.

Interestingly, at the end of the story (Job 42:7–8), God says that Job spoke the truth about God while the friends didn't. They said all the good and holy words found in the psalms and prayers and praise songs. Job, on the other hand, accused God of breaking his word. He said God was hounding him like a hunter stalking a wounded animal, looking for a chance to pump another arrow into his already dying carcass. He accused God of destroying the good right along with the bad. He challenged God to a debate. He portrayed God as wildly free, doing as he pleased with diplomatic immunity from any law. He challenged God to appear in court and offer a defense. He banged on heaven's doors until his knuckles were bloody—but, apparently, no one was at home. Had Job been talking like this in church, we'd have booed him out of the building or had ushers escort him to the atheists' club.

But God said that Job spoke the truth.

Ray Dunning told me one time that the essence of faith is wrestling with God. The word "Israel" probably means "those who wrestle with God." Job is doing well for himself, given his paltry health. He is wrestling with the side of God that he does not understand. Ash-heap theology shoots holes in cause-and-effect religion. God hides and won't appear in court to defend himself, so we do what Job does. We call him out. And according to our story, God is pleased with this action.

I find myself wondering about the conversations in Gethsemane and on the cross. Maybe the essence of faith *is* wrestling with God.

Elie Wiesel, a Holocaust survivor, wrote in his *Memoirs*,
> I have never renounced my faith in God. I have risen against his injustice, protested his silence, and sometimes his absence, but my anger rises up within faith, and not outside it. Prophets and sages rebelled against the lack of divine interference in human affairs during the times of persecution. Abraham, Moses, Jeremiah teach us that it is permissible for a man to accuse God, provided it be done in the name of faith in God. Sometimes we must accept the pain of faith so as not to lose it. And if that makes the tragedy of the believer more devastating than that of the unbeliever, so be it.[2]

A Prayer

Give us a holy uncertainty about our wrong certainties. Deliver us from fixing each other with answers that are non-answers. May we be led by suffering to the heart

---

2. Elie Wiesel, *Memoirs: All Rivers Run to the Sea* (New York: Knopf, 1995), 84.

of God, revealed most clearly on a cross, where God came to us on the ash heap and there died in our place. Amen.

9 THE DARK SIDE OF GOD

C. S. LEWIS is one of the great Christian authors. His writings are creative and honest. When his wife died of cancer, he experienced God in a way he had not before—absent, unexplainable, dark. He recorded his thoughts in what became *A Grief Observed.* He wrote,

Meanwhile, where is God? This is one of the most disquieting symptoms. When you are happy, so happy that you have no sense of needing Him, so happy that you are tempted to feel His claims upon you as an interruption, if you remember yourself and turn to Him with gratitude and praise you will be—or so it feels—welcomed with open arms. But go to Him when your need is desperate, when all other help is vain, and what do you find? A door slammed in your face, and a sound of bolting and double bolting on the inside. After that, silence. You may as well turn away. The longer you wait, the more emphatic the silence will become. There are no lights in the windows. It might be an empty house. Was it ever inhabited? It seemed so once. And that seeming was as strong as this. What can this mean? Why is He so present as a commander in our time of prosperity and so very absent a help in time of trouble?[1]

Where is God? Elie Wiesel, a Jewish teenager during the Holocaust, witnessed the deaths of his family and of his innocence. He wrote of his experiences in *Night*:

I witnessed other hangings. I never saw a single one of the victims weep. For a long time those dried-up bodies had forgotten the bitter taste of tears.

Except once. The Oberkapo of the fifty-second cable unit was a Dutchman, a giant, well over six feet. Seven hundred prisoners worked under his orders, and they all loved him like a brother. No one had ever received a blow at his hands, nor an insult from his lips.

He had a young boy under him—a child with a re-fined and beautiful face, unheard of in this camp. . . . One day, the electric power station at Buna was blown up. The Gestapo, summoned to the spot, suspected sabotage. They found a trail. It eventu-ally led to the Dutch Oberkapo. And there, after a search, they found an important stock of arms.

The Oberkapo was arrested immediately. He was tortured for a period of weeks, but in vain. He would not give a single name. He was transferred to Auschwitz. We never heard of him again. But his little servant had been left behind in the camp in prison. Also put to torture, he too would not speak. Then the SS sentenced him to death, with two other prisoners who had been discovered with arms.

One day when we came back from work, we saw three gallows rearing up in the assembly place, three black crows. Roll call. SS all around us, machine guns trained: the traditional ceremony. Three victims in chains—and one of them, the little servant, the sad-eyed angel.

The SS seemed more preoccupied, more disturbed than usual. To hang a boy in front of thousands of spectators was no light matter. The head of the camp read the verdict. All eyes were on the child. He was lividly pale, almost calm, biting his lips. The gallows threw its shadow over him.

Three victims mounted together onto the chairs.

The three necks were placed at the same moment within the nooses.

"Long live liberty!" cried two adults.

But the child was silent.

"Where is God? Where is He?" someone behind me asked.

At a sign from the head of the camp, the three chairs tipped over.

Total silence throughout the camp. On the horizon, the sun was setting.

We were weeping.

Then the march past began. The two adults were no longer alive. Their tongues swollen, blue-tinged. But the third rope was still moving; being so light, the child was still alive.

For more than half an hour he stayed there, struggling between life and death, dying in slow agony under our eyes. And we had to look him full in the face. He was still alive when I passed in front of him. His tongue was still red, his eyes were not yet glazed.

Behind me, I heard the same man asking: "Where is God now?"

And I heard a voice within me answer him: "Where is He? Here He is—He is hanging here on this gallows."[2]

C. S. Lewis asked it. Elie Wiesel asked it. Job asked it. Even from the cross, Jesus asked it. "My God, my God, why have you forsaken me?" (Matthew 27:46; Mark 15:34, NRSV). Jesus and Job begin to sound vaguely familiar. Listen to these words from Job 29–31, brilliantly paraphrased by Eugene Peterson:

Job now resumed his response:
"Oh, how I long for the good old days, when God took such very good care of me. He always held a lamp before me and I walked through the dark by its light. Oh, how I miss those golden years when God's friendship graced my home, when the Mighty

2. Elie Wiesel, *Night* (New York: Bantam Books, 1983), 60–61.

One was still by my side and my children were all around me, when everything was going my way, and nothing seemed too difficult.

"When I walked downtown and sat with my friends in the public square, young and old greeted me with respect; I was honored by everyone in town. When I spoke, everyone listened; they hung on my every word. People who knew me spoke well of me; my reputation went ahead of me. I was known for helping people in trouble and standing up for those who were down on their luck. The dying blessed me, and the bereaved were cheered by my visits. All my dealings with people were good. I was known for being fair to everyone I met. I was eyes to the blind and feet to the lame, father to the needy, and champion of abused aliens. I grabbed street thieves by the scruff of the neck and made them give back what they'd stolen. I thought, 'I'll die peacefully in my own bed, grateful for a long and full life, a life deep-rooted and well-watered, a life limber and dew-fresh, my soul suffused with glory and my body robust until the day I die.'

"Men and women listened when I spoke, hung expectantly on my every word. After I spoke, they'd be quiet, taking it all in. They welcomed my counsel like spring rain, drinking it all in. When I smiled at them, they could hardly believe it; their faces lit up, their troubles took wing! I was their leader, establishing the mood and setting the pace by which they lived. Where I led, they followed.

"But no longer. Now I'm the butt of their jokes—young ruffians! whippersnappers! Why, I considered their fathers mere inexperienced pups. But they are worse than dogs—good for nothing, stray, mangy animals, half-starved, scavenging the back alleys, howling at the moon; homeless guttersnipes chewing on old bones and licking old tin cans; outcasts from the community, cursed as dangerous delinquents. Nobody would put up with them; they were driven from the neighborhood. You could hear them out there at the edge of town, yelping and barking, huddled in junkyards, a gang of beggars and no-names, thrown out on their ears.

"But now I'm the one they're after, mistreating me, taunting and mocking. They abhor me, they abuse me. How dare those scoundrels—they spit in my face! Now that God has undone me and left me in a heap, they hold nothing back. Anything goes. They come at me from my blind side, trip me up, then jump on me while I'm down. They throw every kind of obstacle in my path, determined to ruin me—and no one lifts a finger to help me! They violate my broken body, trample through the rubble of my ruined life. Terrors assault me—my dignity in shreds, salvation up in smoke.

"And now my life drains out, as suffering seizes and grips me hard. Night gnaws at my bones; the pain never lets up. I am tied hand and foot, my neck in a noose. I twist and turn. Thrown facedown in the muck, I'm a muddy mess, inside and out.

*"I shout for help, God, and get nothing, no answer!
I stand to face you in protest, and you give me a
blank stare! You've turned into my tormenter—you
slap me around, knock me about. You raised me
up so I was riding high and then dropped me, and I
crashed. I know you're determined to kill me, to put
me six feet under.*

*"What did I do to deserve this? Did I ever hit any-
one who was calling for help? Haven't I wept for
those who live a hard life, been heartsick over the
lot of the poor? But where did it get me? I expect-
ed good but evil showed up. I looked for light but
darkness fell. My stomach's in a constant churning,
never settles down. Each day confronts me with
more suffering. I walk under a black cloud. The sun
is gone. I stand in the congregation and protest.
I howl with the jackals, I hoot with the owls. I'm
black-and-blue all over, burning up with fever. My
fiddle plays nothing but the blues; my mouth harp
wails laments.*

*"I made a solemn pact with myself never to undress
a girl with my eyes. So what can I expect from God?
What do I deserve from God Almighty above? Isn't
calamity reserved for the wicked? Isn't disaster
supposed to strike those who do wrong? Isn't God
looking, observing how I live? Doesn't he mark every step I take?*

*"Have I walked hand in hand with falsehood, or
hung out in the company of deceit? Weigh me on a
set of honest scales so God has proof of my integrity. If I've strayed off the straight and narrow, want-*

ed things I had no right to, messed around with sin,
go ahead, then—give my portion to someone who
deserves it.

"If I've let myself be seduced by a woman and con-
spired to go to bed with her, fine, my wife has every
right to go ahead and sleep with anyone she wants
to. For disgusting behavior like that, I'd deserve the
worst punishment you could hand out. Adultery is
a fire that burns the house down; I wouldn't expect
anything I count dear to survive it.

"Have I ever been unfair to my employees when
they brought a complaint to me? What, then, will I
do when God confronts me? When God examines
my books, what can I say? Didn't the same God
who made me, make them? Aren't we all made of
the same stuff, equals before God?

"Have I ignored the needs of the poor, turned my
back on the indigent, taken care of my own needs
and fed my own face while they languished? Wasn't
my home always open to them? Weren't they always welcome at my table?

"Have I ever left a poor family shivering in the cold
when they had no warm clothes? Didn't the poor
bless me when they saw me coming, knowing I'd
brought coats from my closet?

"If I've ever used my strength and influence to take
advantage of the unfortunate, go ahead, break both
my arms, cut off all my fingers! The fear of God has
kept me from these things—how else could I ever
face him?

"Did I set my heart on making big money or worship at the bank? Did I boast about my wealth, show off because I was well-off? Was I ever so awed by the sun's brilliance and moved by the moon's beauty that I let myself become seduced by them and worshiped them on the sly? If so, I would deserve the worst of punishments, for I would be betraying God himself.

"Did I ever crow over my enemy's ruin? Or gloat over my rival's bad luck? No, I never said a word of detraction, never cursed them, even under my breath.

"Didn't those who worked for me say, 'He fed us well. There were always second helpings'? And no stranger ever had to spend a night in the street; my doors were always open to travelers. Did I hide my sin the way Adam did, or conceal my guilt behind closed doors because I was afraid what people would say, fearing the gossip of the neighbors so much that I turned myself into a recluse? You know good and well that I didn't.

"Oh, if only someone would give me a hearing! I've signed my name to my defense—let the Almighty One answer! I want to see my indictment in writing. Anyone's welcome to read my defense; I'll write it on a poster and carry it around town. I'm prepared to account for every move I've ever made—to anyone and everyone, prince or pauper.

"If the very ground that I farm accuses me, if even the furrows fill with tears from my abuse, if I've ever raped the earth for my own profit or dispos-

sessed its rightful owners, then curse it with thistles
instead of wheat, curse it with weeds instead of
barley."

The words of Job to his three friends were finished.

This is the end of Job's speeches. He seems to talk himself into hope, then despair of that very hope the next moment. He asks the God he understands to help him get justice from the God he doesn't understand. He seeks an arbitrator, a mediator, someone to stand between him and God. He seeks a witness who will speak honestly on his behalf. He seeks a kinsman redeemer—a member of his own family—to come to his rescue. He is convinced that, if someone could explain to God his predicament, God would certainly bring justice to bear. It appears he has exhausted all hope of a hearing before God. Job wants justice but can't find anyone to deliver it.

Justice is getting what we deserve, reaping what we sow, fair payment for services rendered, punishment that fits the crime. The good get good, the bad get bad. Job will settle for justice. And Satan thinks that's the way the world runs. God gives humans what we deserve—no more, no less. According to Satan, God is boxed in by these rules. God cannot be merciful to sinners or merciless to saints. God is as predictable as the ATM. He dispenses what we have the right to receive.

But God is not bound by this logic. God knows that Job is capable of loving freely, with a response not coerced by favors. God knows that Job has the capacity to react to divine love freely given. Justice is not cause-and-effect outcome but a world being made right by the love of God.

And in the fullness of time, God came to our ash heap.

As the story unfolds in the Gospel of Mark, Jesus is abandoned. He loses his followers, his legal rights, his health, his dignity, his breath. He is cursed and cast out to die with the criminals and societal rejects on a heap called Calvary. Mark writes, "At noon the sky became extremely dark. The darkness lasted three hours. At three o'clock, Jesus groaned out of the depths, crying loudly, *'Eloi, Eloi, lama sabachthani?'* which means, 'My God, my God, why have you abandoned me?'" (15:33–34).

Jesus died in the dark, crying out to God.

Where is God?

There he is, on a cross. Sovereign, powerful, free to do anything he pleases. Creator, mysterious, unfathomable. But this God dies in our place. Bound by nails, immobile, without hope of tomorrow, a victim of injustice, abandoned on the ash heap of human rejection.

The God who is free to do as he chooses, chooses to receive into himself the injustice of evil because he wishes to be with us in the place where we are abandoned. Elie Wiesel was right. God is here. God is the God of the ash heap.

A Prayer

God of the ash heap, God behind locked and bolted doors, God of no response—maybe when Job cries out to you, maybe when Jesus cries out to you, maybe when we cry out to you and sense that you are absent, maybe you are the cry inside of us. Maybe you are that near and we don't know it. Amen.

10 | THE THIN LINE

SUFFERING gets our attention like nothing else. We are opened wide for wisdom in the places where life has become unbearable. Our prayer life is natural breath rather than intentional practice. Our schedule is open to hear any wise soul that may have answers or help. We are in a liminal state, poised for something new. Like Job, we have nothing else to do but try to figure out where we are, why we are there, and how we move into tomorrow.

We have been led by suffering to a thin line that separates who we are now from who we will be. At this thin line, the visible and invisible bump up against each other, the known and unknown meet, time and eternity kiss. We have shed our arrogance about knowing. We have confessed that we are in over our heads and can't find our way through or out. We ask our best and most honest questions. We are teachable, changeable. And God is at work at this line, even if we don't realize it.

Job comes to this thin line in chapter 28. It is the hinge of the book. He moves from knowing with certainty to not knowing. He now asks God rather than challenging God. Read Job 28 with me:

"We all know how silver seams the rocks, we've seen the stuff from which gold is refined, we're aware of how iron is dug out of the ground and copper is smelted from rock. Miners penetrate the earth's darkness, searching the roots of the mountains for ore, digging away in the suffocating darkness. Far from civilization, far from the traffic, they cut a shaft, and are lowered into it by ropes. Earth's surface is a field for grain, but its depths are a forge firing sapphires from stones and chiseling gold from rocks. Vultures are blind to its riches, hawks never lay eyes on it. Wild animals are oblivious to it, lions don't know it's there. Miners hammer away at the rock, they uproot the mountains. They tunnel through the rock and find all kinds of beautiful gems. They discover the origins of rivers, and bring earth's secrets to light.

"But where, oh where, will they find Wisdom? Where does Insight hide? Mortals don't have a clue, haven't the slightest idea where to look. Earth's depths say, 'It's not here'; ocean deeps echo, 'Never heard of it.' It can't be bought with the finest gold; no amount of silver can get it. Even famous Ophir gold can't buy it, not even diamonds and sapphires. Neither gold nor emeralds are comparable; extravagant jewelry can't touch it. Pearl necklaces and ruby bracelets—why bother? None of this is even a down payment on Wisdom! Pile gold and African

diamonds as high as you will, they can't hold a candle to Wisdom.

"So where does Wisdom come from? And where does Insight live? It can't be found by looking, no matter how deep you dig, no matter how high you fly. If you search through the graveyard and question the dead, they say, 'We've only heard rumors of it.'

"God alone knows the way to Wisdom, he knows the exact place to find it. He knows where everything is on earth, he sees everything under heaven. After he commanded the winds to blow and measured out the waters, arranged for the rain and set off explosions of thunder and lightning, he focused on Wisdom, made sure it was all set and tested and ready. Then he addressed the human race: 'Here it is! Fear-of-the-Lord—that's Wisdom, and Insight means shunning evil.'"

At the thin line, science and technology can't help us. We've mastered the art of digging for iron, copper, and gold. We've dug for sapphire and precious stone. We've tunneled the earth for what lies hidden beneath. And, since the writing of Job 28, we've also split the atom, decoded the gene, cloned an animal, and duplicated cells—but we still cannot fathom suffering.

Only One can create a future through suffering: the God whose breath is wind, whose handclap is thunder, whose finger snap is lightning, whose tears are rain. This creative God comes to the thin line of human suffering clothed in mystery. And we are made capable of receiving revelation. We become frail children, not so wise in our own eyes anymore, not so sure of ourselves, willing to live into a way that we do not fully comprehend.

We fear the Lord—not with a fear that repels but with one that kneels. Like standing at the edge of the Grand Canyon, we shake as we move forward to see the mystery before us, knowing we are in a place where a misstep would be fatal. In The Message, Job calls it 'fear-of-the-Lord—Wisdom.'

A Prayer

At this thin line we seek you with fear-of-the-Lord—Wisdom. We stand here in submissive openness, half wanting to keep arguing with you and demanding of you the answers we think we deserve but also half done with our speeches. We have no other place to go except this thin line because no other creates the future.

11 GOD ANSWERS JOB— MAYBE

GOD HAS BEEN QUIET since the early wager with Satan in the opening chapters. God brags about Job's integrity and then lets it all play out. The hedge is removed, suffering comes, Job sits on an ash heap pondering his plight, friends come to comfort and then to interpret what has transpired, Job makes speeches, they make counter speeches, Job challenges God, they tell him he can't do that, and God is silent.

Finally, Job and his friends are exhausted. He sits, along with his exasperated friends, waiting on an ash heap for God to come. And God does come. But what in the world is God talking about? It sounds more like a lecture on nature than a response to suffering. One would almost think God has his wires crossed and is replying to a child asking how animals and nature were formed. And God does more questioning than answering in Job 38–40:2.

And now, finally, GOD answered Job from the eye of a violent storm. He said:

"Why do you confuse the issue? Why do you talk without knowing what you're talking about? Pull yourself together, Job! Up on your feet! Stand tall! I have some questions for you, and I want some straight answers. Where were you when I created the earth? Tell me, since you know so much! Who decided on its size? Certainly you'll know that! Who came up with the blueprints and measurements? How was its foundation poured, and who set the cornerstone, while the morning stars sang in chorus and all the angels shouted praise? And who took charge of the ocean when it gushed forth like a baby from the womb? That was me! I wrapped it in soft clouds, and tucked it in safely at night. Then I made a playpen for it, a strong playpen so it couldn't run loose, and said, 'Stay here, this is your place. Your wild tantrums are confined to this place.'

"And have you ever ordered Morning, 'Get up!' told Dawn, 'Get to work!' so you could seize Earth like a blanket and shake out the wicked like cockroaches? As the sun brings everything to light, brings out all the colors and shapes, the cover of darkness is snatched from the wicked—they're caught in the very act!

"Have you ever gotten to the true bottom of things, explored the labyrinthine caves of deep ocean? Do you know the first thing about death? Do you have one clue regarding death's dark mysteries? And do you have any idea how large this earth is? Speak up if you have even the beginning of an answer.

"Do you know where Light comes from and where Darkness lives so you can take them by the hand and lead them home when they get lost? Why, of course you know that. You've known them all your life, grown up in the same neighborhood with them!

"Have you ever traveled to where snow is made, seen the vault where hail is stockpiled, the arsenals of hail and snow that I keep in readiness for times of trouble and battle and war? Can you find your way to where lightning is launched, or to the place from which the wind blows? Who do you suppose carves canyons for the downpours of rain, and charts the route of thunderstorms that bring water to unvisited fields, deserts no one ever lays eyes on, drenching the useless wastelands so they're carpeted with wildflowers and grass? And who do you think is the father of rain and dew, the mother of ice and frost? You don't for a minute imagine these marvels of weather just happen, do you?

"Can you catch the eye of the beautiful Pleiades sisters, or distract Orion from his hunt? Can you get Venus to look your way, or get the Great Bear and her cubs to come out and play? Do you know the first thing about the sky's constellations and how they affect things on Earth?

"Can you get the attention of the clouds, and commission a shower of rain? Can you take charge of the lightning bolts and have them report to you for orders?

"Who do you think gave weather-wisdom to the ibis, and storm-savvy to the rooster? Does anyone

know enough to number all the clouds or tip over the rain barrels of heaven when the earth is cracked and dry, the ground baked hard as a brick?

"Can you teach the lioness to stalk her prey and satisfy the appetite of her cubs as they crouch in their den, waiting hungrily in their cave? And who sets out food for the ravens when their young cry to God, fluttering about because they have no food?

"Do you know the month when mountain goats give birth? Have you ever watched a doe bear her fawn? Do you know how many months she is pregnant? Do you know the season of her delivery, when she crouches down and drops her offspring? Her young ones flourish and are soon on their own; they leave and don't come back.

"Who do you think set the wild donkey free, opened the corral gates and let him go? I gave him the whole wilderness to roam in, the rolling plains and wide-open places. He laughs at his city cousins, who are harnessed and harried. He's oblivious to the cries of teamsters. He grazes freely through the hills, nibbling anything that's green.

"Will the wild buffalo condescend to serve you, volunteer to spend the night in your barn? Can you imagine hitching your plow to a buffalo and getting him to till your fields? He's hugely strong, yes, but could you trust him, would you dare turn the job over to him? You wouldn't for a minute depend on him, would you, to do what you said when you said it?

"The ostrich flaps her wings futilely—all those beautiful feathers, but useless! She lays her eggs on the hard ground, leaves them there in the dirt, exposed to the weather, not caring that they might get stepped on and cracked or trampled by some wild animal. She's negligent with her young, as if they weren't even hers. She cares nothing about anything. She wasn't created very smart, that's for sure, wasn't given her share of good sense. But when she runs, oh, how she runs, laughing, leaving horse and rider in the dust.

"Are you the one who gave the horse his prowess and adorned him with a shimmering mane? Did you create him to prance proudly and strike terror with his royal snorts? He paws the ground fiercely, eager and spirited, then charges into the fray. He laughs at danger, fearless, doesn't shy away from the sword. The banging and clanging of quiver and lance don't faze him. He quivers with excitement, and at the trumpet blast races off at a gallop. At the sound of the trumpet he neighs mightily, smelling the excitement of battle from a long way off, catching the rolling thunder of the war cries.

"Was it through your know-how that the hawk learned to fly, soaring effortlessly on thermal updrafts? Did you command the eagle's flight, and teach her to build her nest in the heights, perfectly at home on the high cliff face, invulnerable on pinnacle and crag? From her perch she searches for prey, spies it at a great distance. Her young gorge themselves on carrion; wherever there's a roadkill, you'll see her circling."

GOD then confronted Job directly:

"Now what do you have to say for yourself? Are you going to haul me, the Mighty One, into court and press charges?"

What kind of answer is this to the plight of human suffering? We are treated to a long speech about the frolicking freedom by which God creates the world. Humans are never mentioned. We hear about wild animals that delight God, stars that dance in the sky, weather that services dry deserts, buffalo that don't sleep in barns, darkness that comes and goes without permission.

In essence, we are being told that the world does not revolve around us. We do not make the world go round; God does. And this spinning world is free, not mechanical. Apparently, a free world has the capacity for things to go wrong. No one knows that better than Job.

In this world, the innocent can suffer. And they do. Job loses his business, his children, his health, his reputation, his trust in God—for no apparent fault of his own but for a wager between God and Satan. But that is no more unfair than the thirteen-year-old black teenager who was beaten within an inch of his life just for walking through a white Chicago neighborhood. Or the emergency room physician who contracted AIDS from a frenzied drug addict who slashed him as he tried to save his life. Or the faithful wife of thirty-seven years who was dumped because the decades took a toll on her appearance. In a free world, things can and do go wrong. Hedges don't always hold.

In the speech, God talks *to* us but not *about* us. There is dignity in this. We are the only creature in all of creation who is spoken to, communicated with, invited to know and understand. Satan says we are conditioned to be righteous by God's blessing. God says we are free to respond as we choose. Satan says we are pampered pawns for God's pleasure. God says we are creatures who have choices. Satan says we are conditioned to do good. God says we are made capable of both good and evil.

At the end of God's first speech, we are left with enormous creation questions that we cannot answer, and also with the sense that the world does not revolve around us. Is God putting us in our place, or is this the prelude to a second lecture from our Maker? Job replies to God and then listens again to a speech about a land beast and a sea beast—Behemoth and Leviathan—each larger than life in the mythology of Job's day. They are the beasts of chaos whom God tamed to bring creation into existence. God wants to know if Job can tame them. Take a peek at their conversation in 40:3–41:

Job answered:

> *"I'm speechless, in awe—words fail me. I should never have opened my mouth! I've talked too much, way too much. I'm ready to shut up and listen."*

> *God addressed Job next from the eye of the storm, and this is what he said:*

> *"I have some more questions for you, and I want straight answers.*

"Do you presume to tell me what I'm doing wrong?
Are you calling me a sinner so you can be a saint?
Do you have an arm like my arm? Can you shout in
thunder the way I can? Go ahead, show your stuff.
Let's see what you're made of, what you can do.
Unleash your outrage. Target the arrogant and lay
them flat. Target the arrogant and bring them to
their knees. Stop the wicked in their tracks—make
mincemeat of them! Dig a mass grave and dump
them in it—faceless corpses in an unmarked grave.
I'll gladly step aside and hand things over to you—
you can surely save yourself with no help from me!

"Look at the land beast, Behemoth. I created him
as well as you. Grazing on grass, docile as a cow—
just look at the strength of his back, the powerful
muscles of his belly. His tail sways like a cedar in the
wind; his huge legs are like beech trees. His skele-
ton is made of steel, every bone in his body hard
as steel. Most magnificent of all my creatures, but
I still lead him around like a lamb! The grass-cov-
ered hills serve him meals, while field mice frolic in
his shadow. He takes afternoon naps under shade
trees, cools himself in the reedy swamps, lazily cool
in the leafy shadows as the breeze moves through
the willows. And when the river rages he doesn't
budge, stolid and unperturbed even when the Jor-
dan goes wild. But you'd never want him for a pet—
you'd never be able to housebreak him!

"Or can you pull in the sea beast, Leviathan, with a
fly rod and stuff him in your creel? Can you las-
so him with a rope, or snag him with an anchor?
Will he beg you over and over for mercy, or flatter

you with flowery speech? Will he apply for a job with you to run errands and serve you the rest of your life? Will you play with him as if he were a pet goldfish? Will you make him the mascot of the neighborhood children? Will you put him on display in the market and have shoppers haggle over the price? Could you shoot him full of arrows like a pin cushion, or drive harpoons into his huge head? If you so much as lay a hand on him, you won't live to tell the story. What hope would you have with such a creature? Why, one look at him would do you in! If you can't hold your own against his glowering visage, how, then, do you expect to stand up to me? Who could confront me and get by with it? I'm in charge of all this—I run this universe!

"But I've more to say about Leviathan, the sea beast, his enormous bulk, his beautiful shape. Who would even dream of piercing that tough skin or putting those jaws into bit and bridle? And who would dare knock at the door of his mouth filled with row upon row of fierce teeth? His pride is invincible; nothing can make a dent in that pride. Nothing can get through that proud skin—impervious to weapons and weather, the thickest and toughest of hides, impenetrable!

"He snorts and the world lights up with fire, he blinks and the dawn breaks. Comets pour out of his mouth, fireworks arc and branch. Smoke erupts from his nostrils like steam from a boiling pot. He blows and fires blaze; flames of fire stream from his mouth. All muscle he is—sheer and seamless muscle. To meet him is to dance with death. Sinewy and lithe, *there's not a soft spot in his entire body—as tough inside as out, rock-hard, invulnerable. Even angels run for cover when he surfaces, cowering before his tail-thrashing turbulence. Javelins bounce harmlessly off his hide, harpoons ricochet wildly. Iron bars are so much straw to him, bronze weapons beneath notice. Arrows don't even make him blink; bullets make no more impression than raindrops. A battle ax is nothing but a splinter of kindling; he treats a brandished harpoon as a joke. His belly is armor-plated, inexorable—unstoppable as a barge. He roils deep ocean the way you'd boil water, he whips the sea like you'd whip an egg into batter. With a luminous trail stretching out behind him, you might think Ocean had grown a gray beard! There's nothing on this earth quite like him, not an ounce of fear in that creature! He surveys all the high and mighty—king of the ocean, king of the deep!"*

Why this long lecture about an ancient, mythical super-crocodile? My first read of this text is that God is putting Job in his place. It feels demeaning, demoting, sarcastic, scolding, even belittling. Is God asking Job if he'd like to tackle the monsters of chaos? Could it be that Job's world is wild and fierce and that the only one who has the power to control it is God? Or is it noteworthy that Job is the only creature who has the capacity to receive such revelation from God—the only one who can understand the enormity of the good and evil loosed in the world?

Job now knows that the world will not revolve around his comfort or security, that cause-and-effect religion is too weak for this wild world, that hedges break, that

God allows good and evil to run their course among the righteous and unrighteous without respect for persons.

Job's reply is a confession of trust and promise of loyalty. Apparently the crocodile speech had something in it that brought resolution to Job. If God is both the Creator and Tamer of the crocodile-like Leviathan and Behemoth—the chaos beasts of Canaanite mythology who threaten all existence—then God has the ability to control the world God created. This God of tooth and claw descends to talk with Job about suffering. In a similar way to the Noah story, this same God will become flesh and blood within creation and experience in his own body both tooth and claw in the form of a crucifixion. God stands *with* us in suffering, not above or beyond us.

Job is devoted to God not because he's conditioned, not because he's blessed, not because of the hedge—but because God was right. Job is a man of integrity whose righteousness is authentic. God wins the wager. Satan never appears again in the book of Job. Job's friends are rebuked for the way they spoke about God. And Job speaks of the kind of relationship he now has with God, a relationship that relies not on hearsay but on firsthand knowledge, first-person experience. Check out Job's last words to God in 42:1–6:

Job answered GOD:
"I'm convinced: You can do anything and everything. Nothing and no one can upset your plans. You asked, 'Who is this muddying the water, ignorantly confusing the issue, second-guessing my

purposes?' I admit it. I was the one. I babbled on about things far beyond me, made small talk about wonders way over my head. You told me, 'Listen, and let me do the talking. Let me ask the questions. You give the answers.' I admit I once lived by rumors of you; now I have it all firsthand—from my own eyes and ears! I'm sorry—forgive me. I'll never do that again, I promise! I'll never again live on crusts of hearsay, crumbs of rumor."

A Prayer

When we do not understand you, when your ways in this wild world frighten us, remind us that you are Creator of the beasts that threaten us and that they still are under your sovereignty. While this does not protect us, it does assure us who has the final word. We thank you for revealing yourself to us, even when we walk in darkness. Amen.

PART 3
PSALMS OF LAMENT

There are some psalms we do not read in church. They are an expression of raw human emotion in response to things that make no sense: things like enemies who get away with evil, senseless murder, the absence of God. But these psalms made the editor's cut and have become the prayers of the people of God. While they may not be useful for mundane days, they are ours to pray when darkness seems to hide God's face because, sometimes, God is unexplainable.

12 THE LAMENT OF LOUISE

THEY SAY that absence makes the heart grow fonder. I actually prefer presence. When presence becomes absence, we struggle. Ask the one who just buried a loved one, or the one who moved halfway across the country from family and friends, or two college love-birds separated during Christmas break, or the parent adjusting to an empty nest. Presence is preferred.

Absence cries out in cemeteries, in pillows, in letters, in phone calls, and in prayers. Sometimes the absent one will come back. Sometimes they won't.

Those who have never experienced painful absence are no better comfort than Job's friends. They know the lines, but the lines do not match the experience. Their advice is trite.

"Cheer up."

"You'll get over it."

"There'll be another."

"Get a hobby."

"Let's do lunch sometime."

Or the classic, "I'll be praying for you."

People enduring absence have a hard enough time. Must they also endure a barrage of spiritual clichés?

In Psalm 88, God is the absent one. And the psalm ends without God ever showing up. The psalm is complete with three classic lament moves (verses 1–9, 10–12, and 13–18). Each sequential move grows more intense. The direction of the psalm spirals ever downward. Choice words are selected to express the sinking feeling of abandonment. And the fault of it all is laid at the feet of God. God has put this person in this predicament.

Psalm 88:1–9
God, you're my last chance of the day.
I spend the night on my knees before you.
Put me on your salvation agenda;
take notes on the trouble I'm in.
I've had my fill of trouble;
I'm camped on the edge of **hell**.
I'm written off as a lost cause,
one more statistic, a **hopeless case**.
Abandoned as already **dead**,
one more body in a stack of **corpses**,
And not so much as a **gravestone**—
I'm a **black hole** in oblivion.
You've **dropped** me into a **bottomless pit**,
sunk me in a **pitch-black abyss**.
I'm battered senseless by your rage,

relentlessly pounded by your waves of anger.
You turned my friends against me,
made me horrible to them.
I'm caught in a maze and can't find my way out,
blinded by tears of pain and frustration.
I call to you, GOD; all day I call.
I wring my hands, I plead for help.

There is no mistaking the downward language.
Look at the words in **bold type**: hell, hopeless case,
abandoned, dead, corpses, gravestone, black hole,
dropped, bottomless pit, sunk, pitch-black abyss.

And then the lament begins again, only this time the
vehicle of expression is rhetorical questions. In each
question there is a good word and a bad word. The
good word describes what God is *usually like,* and the
bad word defines life as it is *experienced right now.*

Psalm 88:10–12

Are the dead a live audience for your miracles?
Do ghosts ever join the choirs that praise you?
Does your love make any difference in a graveyard?
Is your faithful presence noticed in the corridors of
hell?
Are your marvelous wonders ever seen in the dark,
your righteous ways noticed in the Land of No
Memory?

The assumed answer to each question is no! And then
comes the last sequential move of the psalm. The emotions are uncorked, the words unvarnished. The gloves
are off. You feel the distance deepen between God and
the person praying. And the psalm fittingly ends with
the word "darkness."

Psalm 88:13–18

I'm standing my ground, God, shouting for help,
at my prayers every morning, on my knees each
daybreak.
Why, God, do you turn a deaf ear?
Why do you make yourself scarce?
For as long as I remember I've been hurting;
I've taken the worst you can hand out, and I've had it.
Your wildfire anger has blazed through my life;
I'm bleeding, black-and-blue.
You've attacked me fiercely from every side,
raining down blows till I'm nearly dead.
You made lover and neighbor alike dump me;
the only friend I have left is Darkness.

You almost expect to hear Simon and Garfunkel croon, "Hello, darkness, my old friend. I've come to talk with you again." And why not? It does not appear that God is participating in this conversation. This is one psalm that does not end with "and they all lived happily ever after."

———

I couldn't help Louise. Her saintly Methodist mother was brutally beaten, raped, robbed, and murdered in the house where Louise grew up. Months after the funeral Louise came to me with a wintry heart: cold, empty, emotionless. I was her young, wet-behind-the-ears, fresh-out-of-seminary pastor. I feebly tried to defend and explain the God who had abandoned her and her mother. I wish I had known then what I know now about the function of lament in Scripture and in life. All the time, I was trying to act like there were answers for these things, that God was on the throne and all was right in the world. I was faking it. To be frank, I was perturbed to be caught between her accusations and God's defense.

And I missed the miracle before my eyes.

Here she was, feeling abandoned and cut off by God—yet she kept coming to church, expressing her pain, searching her scriptures, questioning God, banging on the heavenly door, provoking Yahweh, demanding that her covenant partner act like a covenant partner. The miracle was that she didn't leave. She was faithful to the God who abandoned her. She was a better Christian than I was.

If Louise were writing Psalm 88, I think it would sound like this.

The Lament of Louise

God, the nights are hardest.
I feel so lonely.
It is absence.
Not the absence of one whose friend moved to California,
nor the absence of lovers separated for a summer,
nor the absence of an empty nest.
My absence is the cemetery kind.
She won't come back.
Mom is dead.

I knew she'd die one day.
That's okay.

But what kind of world permits the rape and murder of a Bible-believing, flower-raising Methodist mother?

What kind of *God* permits the rape and murder of a Bible-believing, flower-raising Methodist mother?

It's been a year now.
He got a life sentence.
Against my beliefs, I wanted him to fry.
Now I hear he's got jailhouse religion.
He made my earth hell—now my heaven too.
I can't escape him unless I choose hell for myself—
which isn't out of the question right now.

I've been to see the wise ones who preach from the book.
Their advice is trite.
"She's with Jesus now," they say.
But she's not with me.
"She's home," they say.
But that little yellow house has chalk outlines, blood-stain remover, a For Sale sign.
"Read this book. It will help you," they say.
But will it bring justice to earth? Will it erase rape? Will it cure hate?

It didn't use to be like this between us.
It was easy to pray. It was simple to believe.
Now I have to remember her eighty-three years through the lens of one bloody moment.
And I have to share the only haven left—which you call heaven—with a forgiven rapist, a murderer walking down the golden streets just a few feet behind Mom and me.

Where are you in all this?
You're absent.
Out of reach.
I feel so lonely.
God, the nights are hardest.

Sometimes the only authentic form faith can take is a complaint about absence. And for those who believe in God, when comes the dark night of the soul, when winter settles in the heart, when passion vacates the emotions, when happy songs are empty acts—the cry of absence is the only presence of God.

If I were still Louise's pastor, I would say to her now, "You amaze me. You have, quite possibly, the strongest faith I've ever seen. Most people would give up on God, but here you are, still waiting, still praying, still hoping. Where did you get such a faith?"

And she might say, "From the one who died, abandoned, on the cross."

13 ENEMIES

ENEMIES are out there. They will hurt us if they can. At times they are cold and arrogant. They usually fight sideways or attack from the rear. Their goal is to shame, embarrass, discredit, or harm, and they will seize any available opportunity to do so. Their words are poison. Their compliments are backhanded. Their good deeds are laced with razor blades. Our success is their worst nightmare. Our failure is their cherished dream. They can be shrewd, look civil, and pass for moral. They are often deeply angry, insecure, or afraid, but they don't always know it or aren't capable of admitting it. They come in all shapes and sizes. Enemies are out there.

In Psalm 109, an enemy has struck. The psalmist opens his heart wide enough for us to watch him process his pain. For those who think the Bible is a bland, controlled book, think again. This is raw. Our friend begins: "Do not be silent, O God of my praise. For wicked and deceitful mouths are opened against me, speaking against me with lying tongues. They beset me with words of hate, and attack me without cause. In return for my love they accuse me, even while I make prayer for them. So they reward me evil for good, and hatred for my love" (vv. 1-5, NRSV).

This is standard operating procedure. This type of psalm is called a lament, and the writer is following the form to the letter. A structured lament

A) addresses God,
B) brings a complaint to God and tells what the enemy did, and
C) calls on God to save the writer from the enemy.

To write a lament is to deal with the enemy by the book: Enemy 101.

I understand why a structured lament is necessary. When something horrible happens and our world is threatened, it is good to have a ritual response that requires no thought. There is not always time for creativity or thoughtfulness. We just need to act. Ritual is a better reaction than rage. Keep it simple: A, call on God; B, complain to God; C, ask God to save you. The structure keeps us from going off half-cocked. Our friend is following the form. But then something snaps. He explodes. Rage erupts inside him. He unloads. He says things we'd never say in church. Check out the rest of Psalm 109 in verses 6-20 of the NRSV:

Appoint a wicked man against him;
let an accuser stand on his right.
When he is tried, let him be found guilty;
let his prayer be counted as sin.

May his days be few; may another seize his position.
May his children be orphans,
and his wife a widow.
May his children wander about and beg;
may they be driven out of the ruins they inhabit.
May the creditor seize all that he has;
may strangers plunder the fruits of his toil.
May there be no one to do him a kindness,
nor anyone to pity his orphaned children.
May his posterity be cut off;
may his name be blotted out in the second generation.
May the iniquity of his father be remembered before the Lord,
and do not let the sin of his mother be blotted out.
Let them be before the Lord continually,
and may his memory be cut off from the earth.
For he did not remember to show kindness,
but pursued the poor and needy and the brokenhearted to their death.
He loved to curse; let curses come on him.
He did not like blessing; may it be far from him.
He clothed himself with cursing as his coat,
may it soak into his body like water,
like oil into his bones.
May it be like a garment that he wraps around himself,
like a belt that he wears every day.
May that be the reward of my accusers from the Lord,
of those who speak evil against my life.

Can you imagine hearing this in a testimony meeting? Someone stands to his feet and begins, "Pastor, I have something to share with the church this morning. Someone lied about me this week. I went to them and tried to make it right and they spit in my face. I've had it with this guy. This is the last straw. I am sick and tired of being walked on by him. I hope he loses his job, gets hauled into court, gets sued into bankruptcy, and sentenced to do time. I hope he dies prematurely and leaves his wife and kids nothing. I hope his aging parents die of heartbreak and shame. I hope the bank forecloses on his mortgage, seizes his assets, and runs a front-page article in the newspaper telling everybody what a jerk he is. I hope every evil deed he has done to people gets done to him and that people spit when they hear his name until the day he dies. And I love the Lord and want to serve him all the days of my life and dwell in the house of the Lord forever. Amen." Wouldn't that be a service to remember!

What is this psalm doing in the Bible? I'll tell you why it's there. This is how humans honestly feel when an enemy intentionally hurts us. It is a normal response to being deeply and repeatedly wronged. We get hurt. And we want God to join us in our vengeance. We believe God has a dark side, like ours, and that God will get us some just payback. Admittedly, our feelings may not possess the same level of octane as our friend in Psalm 109. He lived in a savage world of ethnic cleaning and massacre, a world without jails where ancient justice was swift and on the spot, an eye for an eye and a tooth for a tooth. Revenge was routine, commonplace.

But is it wrong to want revenge for wrong done? Apparently not. God does. More than once God announces that God will carry out vengeance (see Genesis 4:15; Leviticus 26:25; Numbers 31:3; Deuteronomy 32:35, 41; Isaiah 35:4; 47:3). God is a God who desires justice, who works to destroy evil, and who speaks of consequences for wrongdoing. God does not sweep evil under a cosmic rug, look the other way, or ignore perpetrators. God declares that revenge is divine domain. And that's an important point. God will get revenge. It is God's prerogative—which is a hard thing to say about our loving God

In the middle of Psalm 109, the writer has stopped calling on God and started taking matters into his own hands. The avalanche is beginning. He is swearing himself in as judge, jury, and executioner. Of course, we can understand why he's doing this. God seems to be clumsy and slow at revenge. Criminals walk. Cheaters win. Loose lips sink ships. Abusers go free. Our enemies walk away without so much as a slap on the wrist. That's why we take revenge into our own hands. We are better at it—or so we think.

But what do we do with the cross of Jesus? God becomes flesh and takes upon himself our sin, our evil. Love absorbs enemy behavior. He loves not only those who love him—he loves enemies too. If suffering love absorbs wrongdoing, how does justice ever get done? How does God deal with evil?

Let's revisit our Psalm-writing friend. The final verses of Psalm 109:21–31 (NRSV):

But you, O Lord my Lord,
act on my behalf for your name's sake;
because your steadfast love is good, deliver me.
For I am poor and needy,
and my heart is pierced within me.
I am gone like a shadow at evening;
I am shaken off like a locust.
My knees are weak through fasting;
my body has become gaunt.
I am an object of scorn to my accusers;
when they see me, they shake their heads.

Help me, O Lord my God!
Save me according to your steadfast love.
Let them know that this is your hand;
you, O Lord, have done it.
Let them curse, but you will bless.
Let my assailants be put to shame; may your servant be glad.
May my accusers be clothed with dishonor;
may they be wrapped in their own shame as in a mantle.
With my mouth I will give great thanks to the Lord;
I will praise him in the midst of the throng.
For he stands at the right hand of the needy,
to save them from those who would condemn them to death.

Our friend is now back to the ritual formula again—praying that all will see what the enemy has done and learn from it, entrusting the enemy into the hands of God, asking God to vindicate him.

I suppose that is the only way to walk away clean: put our enemies in the hands of God and trust God to do what is just and loving and right. In the process, we are delivered from living enemy-centered lives, from the internal acid of revenge, and from a life of retaliation. But is there enough darkness or light in God to get justice?

Enemies are out there. They have done things to you that are not right. What will you do with this? Psalm 109 points the way. Name the enemy, state the wrong done, pour out your anger to God, seek to have the wrong publicly recognized to keep others from suffering the same sins, put them in God's hands, leave them there, and ask God to vindicate you.

Who knows? In God's hands, miracles happen. You may even come to love your enemy.

14 PROVOKING GOD

DO YOU KNOW how to provoke a response? My wife does. If she's talking and I'm not listening, she turns toward the wall and says, "Why thank you, wall. It's so enjoyable to converse with you today. I delight in these one-way conversations. I can hear the sound of my own lovely voice bouncing back to me."

She's provoking a response. I suppose we learned this tactic from the Old West, when one gunslinger would stand in the street outside the saloon and yell to another gunslinger inside the saloon, "Cactus Jack, I'm calling you out!" He's provoking a response. Teens slam doors or sulk to get a response. Children throw tantrums. Spouses complain or pout. Church members write anonymous notes. Pastors whine in their sermons. Coaches glare at referees. Lovers clam up. All in quest of a response.

We find good company in Psalm 77. Someone is provoking God to respond to their dark, desperate situation. It begins with an emotive gush: "I yell out to my God, I yell with all my might, I yell at the top of my lungs. He listens. I found myself in trouble and went looking for my Lord; my life was an open wound that wouldn't heal. When friends said, 'Everything will turn out all right,' I didn't believe a word they said" (vv. 1–3).

What's the problem? We don't know. That's what I like about these lament psalms: they are fill-in-the-blank-prayers. I can insert my own trouble. And we have plenty, don't we? Loss of people we love. A cutback at work. Alzheimer's. Moving to a town you hate. A kid going bad. A business going under. A deep loneliness. A painful memory that camps on the front door of our consciousness. A marriage getting uglier by the day. A checkbook bleeding red. A relationship that ended when we didn't want it to. The shooting on the evening news. Another bomb in another town. A political decision that adds one more brick to the crippling weight we already bear. We know trouble. Strangely, nobody—yet everybody—knows the trouble we've seen.

Psalm 77 has been where we live. Psalm 77 is a prayer uttered in the dark. And the provoker wants God to pay attention. Notice that she does not address God directly but whines and complains in the presence of God, sure that God is overhearing the diatribe: "I remember God—and shake my head. I bow my head—then wring my hands. I'm awake all night—not a wink of sleep; I can't even say what's bothering me. I go over the days one by one, I ponder the years gone by. I strum my lute all through the night, wondering how to get my life together. Will the Lord walk off and leave us for good? Will he never smile again? Is his love worn threadbare? Has his salvation promise burned out? Has God forgotten his manners? Has he angrily stalked off and left us? 'Just my luck,' I said. 'The High God goes out of business just the moment I need him'" (vv. 4–10).

Do you ever pray like this? Probably not. We are taught to make nice with God in our prayers, to say the floweriest things, to praise like King David. We'd never suggest in our prayer that God has left us in the lurch, or worn us out, or forgotten his manners. We don't stand in front of the Holy of Holies and call God out to meet us at high noon on Main Street. This kind of attitude toward God is unsettling for everybody. The saints get very uncomfortable around these kinds of prayers.

But friends, this prayer and about thirty others like it are in our Bible. These prayers made the editor's cut. And across the years, I've come to be very glad these prayers are there because sometimes—mostly when I'm in trouble—I wonder if God is paying attention. I think the reason we pray like this is not that we don't have faith but that we *do*. Faithless people don't bother to pray. Faithful people believe that God responds to our cry. So we call him out. We say these things because we are sure God is listening—just as sure as the teenager who mutters under her breath, confident that Mom is listening.

I suppose the epitome of the prayer is the conclusion: "Just my luck. The High God goes out of business just the moment I need him." I've been with people who have reached this conclusion. It usually comes after they have prayed a lot, believed a lot, provoked a lot, offered God deals in exchange for a resolution of their trouble, and waited a lot. And nothing happens. Then they announce to me that God has gone out of business. God doesn't answer prayer anymore. I don't think they truly believe this—I certainly don't. I think they just need another believer to hear their provocation and to respond in God's place to assure them that the God who seems absent isn't actually absent.

My response is stories. I have never argued with these kinds of prayers, as if I could talk someone into changing their mind about feeling abandoned by God. I just say, "Life takes us to places like this, doesn't it?" And then I tell stories.

About my sister Vickie, whose daughter Heidi was pronounced terminal at birth by all the doctors, and how the doctors kept telling the family to prepare my sister for the death of her baby, and how Vickie insisted that God was healing her and how Heidi kept holding on and today is healthy as a horse.

About Mark and Christy and how their baby boy died and how we carried his casket across a frozen Chicago cemetery and buried it in the tiniest hole you could imagine, and how they thought life was over for them, and how today they have twins who are the joy of their life.

About Kyle Funke, a college student with deadly cancer, and how his friends prayed and how he kept going to Vanderbilt Hospital for chemotherapy in the morning and showing up in classes the same afternoon and how he died and we cried with his family.

Telling stories helps. It's what happens to our friend in Psalm 77: "Once again I'll go over what GOD has done, lay out on the table the ancient wonders; I'll ponder all the things you've accomplished, and give a long, loving look at your acts. O God! Your way is holy! No god is great like God! You're the God who makes things happen; you showed everyone what you can do—You pulled your people out of the worst kind of trouble, rescued the children of Jacob and Joseph" (vv. 11–15).

Do you recognize that story? It is the story of the Exodus. The people of God are slaves under Pharaoh, crying out to God for deliverance from their harsh taskmaster. While they cry out, unbeknownst to them, God is having a conversation with Moses at a burning bush. God announced to Moses, "I have heard the cries of my people in Egypt" (see Exodus 3:7 of any translation). Of all the depictions of God in Scripture, I like this one best. God hears our cries. When we are down in Egypt, we don't think God hears us because we can't see anything happening. We are wilting under our fill-in-the-blank trouble, and there is no sign of heavenly attention being paid to us. Part of me still believes that we can't hear God because it is God inside of us who is crying out.

I remember praying for my friends Ron and Janet Benefiel. Ron was the president of Nazarene Theological Seminary when his wife, Janet, had a scare with cancer. After battling it for a couple of years, she was pronounced clean and cancer-free. Then it came back—in both lungs and in her ribs. She started chemo again. Ron resigned his role at the seminary, and he and Janet moved back west to be closer to the rest of their family and so Ron could care for her until she eventually passed away.

Ron told me that lots of people sent him the Romans 8:28 promise that God is at work in everything for the good of those who love him. But he said he found more comfort in Romans 8:26: "Meanwhile, the moment we get tired in the waiting, God's Spirit is right alongside helping us along. If we don't know how or what to pray, it doesn't matter. He does our praying in and for us, making prayer out of our wordless sighs, our aching groans." God is in the cry.

Our Old Testament story friends are crying out to God in Egypt, and God is talking to Moses in Midian. As the story unfolds, Pharaoh is no match for the God of troubled people, and they end up headed toward the promised land with all the wealth of Egypt in their backpacks. Then Pharaoh changes his mind and pursues them. I think this action provokes God because a miracle happens at the sea. "Ocean saw you in action, God, saw you and trembled with fear; Deep Ocean was scared to death. Clouds belched buckets of rain, Sky exploded with thunder, your arrows flashing this way and that. From Whirlwind came your thundering voice, Lightning exposed the world, Earth reeled and rocked. You strode right through Ocean, walked straight through roaring Ocean, but nobody saw you come or go. Hidden in the hands of Moses and Aaron, You led your people like a flock of sheep" (Psalm 77:16–20).

And that's how Psalm 77 ends. There is no recorded resolution and no answer from God—only a story about the time they were between Pharaoh's army and the deep blue sea, and God turned the world upside down to create a way through. Apparently, remembering the faithfulness of God in the past got this psalmist through the trouble of the present.

Is a story enough for you? Maybe a story like the one we are headed toward during Holy Week when Jesus hangs abandoned on a cross and prays another Old Testament lament, "My God, my God, why have you forsaken me?" (see Psalm 22:1; Matthew 27:46; Mark 15:34, NRSV).

Sooner or later, life takes us to dark places. And we, like those who have been there before us, wonder, *Where is God?* The Hebrew children down in Egypt asked it. Noah, waiting for rain to stop, asked it. Job on the ash heap asked it. Psalmists in trouble asked it. Jews marching into gas ovens asked it. African slaves in the bottom of ships asked it. Mothers with bombs raining down on their babies asked it. Egyptians and Libyans and Yemeni have asked it. Immigrants being separated from their children ask it. Parents of drug-addicted teens ask it. The poor ask it. Innocent prisoners ask it. Victims of violence ask it. Diseased bodies ask it. Depressed minds ask it. And sometimes you and I ask it. *Where is God?*

To be in the dark is hard, but to be in the dark alone is almost unbearable. Mark's Gospel tells us that Jesus died in the dark. The Gospel story peels away layer after layer of his followers until he is left with the execution experts and the taunting tormentors. Jesus recites Psalm 22, asking the same question we do. Jesus has done nothing to deserve this. He has simply obeyed the Father—which tells me that we can follow God and end up in places similar to the cross.

Some have interpreted the abandonment of Jesus on the cross as God turning his back on Jesus: because Jesus bears the sin of the world and the holy God cannot bear to look upon sin, God looks the other way. I've been with parents in birthing rooms whose babies were born with visible disabilities, and I've never seen them look away. I don't think love looks away from the beloved because of something that is hard to see. This just doesn't sound like God to me.

There are all kinds of atonement theories. For a while, I was a little embarrassed that I didn't subscribe to one. All those years in seminary and I couldn't get my heart around any of the atonement theories. I knew them well.

The substitutionary theory says that Jesus dies so we don't have to. And I suppose that's true.

The moral influence theory says that Jesus died as an example of God's love and that we should be inspired as a result to follow his example and lay down our own lives in love. And I think that's true too.

The penal satisfaction theory says that Jesus took the beating for our sins to appease the anger of God and satisfy our debt. And I can take you to scriptures that seem to say this. But I really don't like this one.

The *Christus Victor* theory says that in the cross and resurrection, God overcame Satan and death. I like this one the most, but it doesn't say everything that I think is being said from Golgotha.

Then one Easter I was working on these psalms of lament, prayers out of the darkness, and I understood something about God, and about Jesus on the cross. In Jesus, God has gone to the places where we go. He goes to the dark places, the places where life is being taken from us, the places where we feel abandoned, the places where we die. And hanging there in our place (or even better, in all the places where we are hung to die), he prays this prayer for us, and he knows how we feel because he went there on our behalf. The cross of Jesus is God's way of saying, "I am there with you, even when you don't know it. I am the cry rising within you, even when you experience me as absent. You will never go to a place that I have not already been. Look in the darkness and you will find my foot-prints. I have prayed for you. I am with you."

This understanding changes the way I pray, especially in the dark. A few years ago, I was thinking about my mother and wrote this:

This is her last night in her home of the past forty-six years. Tomorrow morning she will be lovingly escorted to the East McComb Nursing Home where the last chapter of her life will begin. None of us know how long or short that chapter will be. Dad is eighty-six, in relatively good health, and tired. He has cared for her as long as he could. Tonight he will sleep with her. Tomorrow night he will sleep by himself, alone for the first time in sixty years.

His questions have been fair. Why? Why her? Why now? Why this? Mom has spent her life in service to God and the church: pianist, church treasurer, Sunday school teacher, maker of Kool-Aid for sixty years' worth of Vacation Bible Schools. Couldn't have happened to a finer woman, but it did happen to her. Dad's prayers, which have moved mountains across decades, did not budge this one. Alzheimer's came, and has kept on coming.

Dad keeps asking me why. I'm a pastor and am supposed to have answers for questions like this. He is grieving and feels alone and abandoned. He said the house is very dark at night. Will God come to him in the dark? Will God hear his prayers?

And Mom—does God go to nursing homes? Can God come to one whose grasp of history is fading, to one who cannot recall the Bible stories that have shaped her, to one who will soon wonder who the people are who are smiling at her?

I am a trained theologian; I am not looking for a full-blown theodicy. I have preached sermons to people with my own questions and even written books to answer them. I know the answers. Religion—good religion—is loaded with very helpful answers. Bad religion isn't worth the effort. But what I hope for my mother and father is not answers but presence—the presence of God in the East McComb Nursing Home.

And so, the psalmist prays:
Is there anyplace I can go to avoid your Spirit?
to be out of your sight?
If I climb to the sky, you're there!
If I go underground, you're there!
If I flew on morning's wings
to the far western horizon,
You'd find me in a minute—
You're already there waiting!

Then I said to myself, "Oh, he even sees me in the dark!
At night I'm immersed in the light!"
It's a fact: darkness isn't dark to you;
night and day, darkness and light, they're all the same to you.
(Psalm 139:7–12)

The next time you ask God where he is, remember that Jesus is the voice inside you asking.

AFTERWORD

BARBARA BROWN TAYLOR shares the following story in her excellent article on "Preaching the Terrors."

Several summers ago, I spent three days on a barrier island where loggerhead turtles were laying their eggs. One night while the tide was out, I watched a huge female heave herself up the beach to dig her nest and empty herself into it while slow, salt tears ran from her eyes. Afraid of disturbing her, I left before she had finished her work but returned next morning to see if I could find the spot where her eggs lay hidden in the sand. What I found were her tracks, only they led in the wrong direction. Instead of heading out to sea, she had wandered into the dunes, which were already hot as asphalt in the morning sun.

A little ways inland I found her, exhausted and all but baked, her head and flippers caked with dried sand. After pouring water on her and covering her with sea oats, I fetched a park ranger, who returned with a jeep to rescue her. As I watched in horror, he flipped her over on her back, wrapped tire chains around her front legs, and hooked the chains to the trailer hitch on his Jeep. Then he took off, yanking her body forward so fast that her open mouth filled with sand and then disappeared underneath her as her neck bent so far I feared it would break.

The ranger hauled her over the dunes and down onto the beach; I followed the path that the prow of her shell cut in the sand. At ocean's edge, he unhooked her and turned her right side up again. She lay motionless in the surf as the water lapped at her body, washing the sand from her eyes and making her skin shine again.

Then a particularly large wave broke over her, and she lifted her head slightly, moving her back legs as she did. As I watched, she revived. Every fresh wave brought her life back to her until one of them made her light enough to find a foothold and push off, back into the water that was her home.

Watching her swim slowly away and remembering her nightmare ride through the dunes, I noted that it is sometimes hard to tell whether you are being killed or saved by the hands that turn your life upside down.[1]

1. Barbara Brown Taylor, "Preaching the Terrors," *Leadership Journal* (Spring 1992), 45. *Leadership Journal* was published by *Christianity Today*, where the article's archive can be found: https://www.christianitytoday.com/pastors/1992/spring/9212042.html.